How to Study

Kenneth E. Standley

DALE SEYMOUR PUBLICATIONS

Cover design: Gail Blackmarr
Cartoons: Dick Davies
Figures and lettering: Susan Cronin-Paris

Originally published by the Study Skills Institute of California as a
series of six booklets, © 1981 by Kenneth E. Standley.

Order number DS13703
ISBN 0-86651-356-6

DALE
SEYMOUR
PUBLICATIONS
P.O. BOX 10888
PALO ALTO, CA 94303

6 7 8 9 10 11 12 13 14 15-MA-95 94 93 92 91

Contents

Part 1
Vital Information   1
The End
The Future Is Your Responsibility
You Usually Do Not Reach Someone
    Else's Goals
You Have Been Selected

Part 2
How to Manage Your Time   13
You Cannot Manage Time
You Needn't Be a Slave to the Clock
How Do You Use Your Time?
Time Diary Exercise
Making a Daily Plan
You Are the General Manager of Your Life
Goofing Off with Style and Effectiveness
A Successful Life Starts with Successful
    Minutes
Go For It!

Part 3
How to Take Notes in Class   35
Using Speed Writing
Common Questions and Misconceptions
    About Note Taking
Don't Give Your Mind Excused Absences
    from Class
The Computer Every Student Can Use
The Ancient Method of Remembering
The Memory-Key Method
Don't Write Down Everything That's Said
Selecting Memory Keys
Memory Key Practice Exercises
Practice for Taking Notes in Class

Part 4
How to Study Your Textbook   69
A Winner Has to Be Only a Little Better
Getting Ready to Study
It's Not Necessary to Read a Textbook
    Again and Again
The Professional Way to Study Your
    Textbook
The TI-3R Method
Textbook Study Practice Exercises

Part 5
How to Study for Tests   97
Studying for Test Success
Don't Be a Counterfeiter
Solitaire Lay-Down Cards
Deal Yourself an "A"
Other Good Ways to Use Solitaire
    Lay-Down Cards
Good Study Methods Prevent the
    Loser's Limp

Part 6
How to Take Tests   115
The Splashdown Method for Taking Tests
Splashdown Practice Exercises
Emotional and Physical Preparation
    for an Exam
Improving Concentration During a Test
Objective Tests: Plan Your Strategy
Essay Tests: Students Have the Advantage
Your Corrected Test Is Valuable
The Beginning

Answer Key   139

Part 1

Vital Information

Perhaps the most valuable result of education
is the ability to make yourself do the thing
you have to do, when it ought to be done,
whether you want to or not. It is the first lesson
that must be learned.

—Thomas Huxley

The End

This is the end—not the end of the book, but the end of having to use hit-and-miss techniques for studying.

We all know the obvious reasons for learning study skills. With these skills we can earn better grades, and even have more free time in the long run to enjoy ourselves. But after careful consideration, you may conclude that there are even more important reasons for learning how to study. Let's think about some of those reasons.

Most of us spend at least twelve years in school. During those years we develop a sense of our personal abilities and form our self-image. That self-image usually stays with us throughout life. The self-confidence, or lack of confidence, that we develop while in school follows us into the working world. In other words, our degree of success or failure in later life often mirrors our success or failure in school. Since the school years set the trend for our future quality of life, the time spent learning skills that can help us succeed is very important.

Many bright students perform below their potential simply because they lack good study skills. There are literally tens of thousands of students who have the ability to become engineers, dentists, lawyers, doctors, business executives, or anything they choose. Some make it, but many accept a job that is not fulfilling and rewarding. Why? Because they have no self-confidence. They believe they lack ability. After all, since they had to struggle to earn passing grades in school, what else are they to believe?

If you have started to lose confidence in your academic performance, don't be too hasty in judging yourself. If you work and slave, but your efforts are not rewarded with the results you want, don't be discouraged. Perhaps you're like the woodcutter whose production kept going down because he didn't take the time to sharpen his ax. In all likelihood, you can increase your production in school (that is, improve your grades) simply by sharpening your study skills.

There are only five basic skills that any of us must learn in order to be successful academically. To be sure, there are many more skills that you must learn eventually. But if you learn these five basic skills, you will be able to adapt, adjust, and expand them to handle any academic challenges you face. These five skills are as follows:

1. Managing time and setting priorities.

2. Listening and taking notes in class—notes that can help with studying later.

3. Reading and understanding a textbook without having to read it again and again.

4. Condensing and organizing material to study for a test.

5. Taking tests successfully.

When you master these five skills, then use and practice them until they become second nature, you will be well on your way to academic excellence.

Keep in mind, however, that if you have been experiencing some difficulties as a student, you cannot improve just by making a casual decision to do so. Improvement involves more than mastering a set of five new skills. You see, over the years you have formed a vivid mental picture of yourself as a certain kind of student. When you decide to change, to improve that picture, you'll find it a lot easier if there's solid evidence that your old mental picture of yourself wasn't quite right and a new, more positive one would be more accurate.

You change that mental picture of yourself to a positive one by demonstrating that you *can* be successful. As you learn to use the five basic study skills and see the effect on your performance, you will begin to believe in the unique abilities you possess.

After a reasonable length of time you will see a more confident, more successful "you" begin to emerge.

Starting a project to improve your study skills is important, but carrying that project through to completion is even more important. That is what will give you the skills to continue succeeding in life. Remember, you add nothing to the score by stopping at third base. Once you have learned the five basic skills, you must make a commitment to practice and develop them. They must become so natural that you no longer think about them consciously.

Let's make this the end—the end of hit-and-miss studying and the end of settling for less than you deserve from your education and from your life.

Questions for Discussion

1. "Our degree of success or failure in life often mirrors our success or failure in school." What does this statement mean?

2. Most students have the ability to become anything they choose. Yet many students accept a job when they get out of school that is not fulfilling or rewarding. Discuss some reasons why this happens.

3. "Perhaps you're like the woodcutter whose production kept going down because he didn't take the time to sharpen his ax." Explain how that applies to you as a student.

4. What are the five basic study skills?

5. Improving as a student means more than just learning a new set of skills. What else is involved?

6. "You add nothing to the score by stopping at third base." What does this statement mean as it applies to improving your study skills?

> There is nothing so fatal to character as half-finished tasks.
> —John Barrymore

Your Future Is Your Responsibility

As a student, you are important. You are special. All students, regardless of age, possess a unique quality that makes them attractive. What is that quality?

It's difficult to identify the quality that sets students apart, but perhaps it's that they are growing. Not all students are still growing physically, of course, but all are growing mentally. The blossoming of potential is encouraging—it makes the future seem brighter. Being a student is being full of potential. But just as physical growth must be nurtured, so too must mental growth.

Some students fail to nurture their mental growth. Instead of exercising and stretching their minds, they look for someone or something to blame when they have problems. They try to shift the responsibility for their problems to someone or something else.

It's really not very difficult to place blame in today's complex society. It's convenient to blame schools and teachers, or parents, or society, or lack of opportunity. When things aren't going well, it's not hard to blame handicaps, environment, ethnic background, race, age, or weight. But ask yourself, "What good does it do to place the blame somewhere else for my problems?" If you point an accusing finger of blame elsewhere and say "It's not my fault," you're using a "loser's limp." What's a loser's limp? Perhaps it can best be explained with this story.

Imagine that you're at a track meet. The crowd buzzes with excitement as the mile race, the most glamorous event of the day, is announced. The stands are packed with hundreds of expectant fans. The gun sounds and the race begins. Through the first lap the runners are tightly bunched. They approach the half-mile mark and the field begins to spread out. At the end of the third lap, two of the strongest runners pull ahead of the pack. With one lap to go, these two fine athletes are running shoulder to shoulder. Their legs are pumping stride for stride. They round the last turn. The crowd stands, cheering wildly, as the runners sprint for the finish line. Suddenly, one runner begins to lose ground. There's still time for him to pull it out, to win, but instead of being spurred on by the challenge, he panics. He thinks, "Oh no! I'm going to lose! I'm going to be embarrassed

in front of all these people!" Instead of digging in for the finish line and a winning surge, he looks for an excuse. He looks for something to blame.

What does he do? He develops a limp. He knows that everyone in the stands will understand why he lost if they think he pulled a muscle. They will think he really tried, that it wasn't his fault. They will understand that the limp cost him the victory.

The sad part of this story is that even though the runner may have an excuse, he still lost. His loser's limp cost him the drive for the finish line that might have brought him victory. It kept him out of the winner's circle.

When things are going less then perfectly for you, don't look for someone to blame. Your success and your future are in *your* hands. Of course, you will need the help of a good education to fully develop your future. All of us do. But you are the only one who can use your ability. It's a big and exciting responsibility, and it belongs to you alone.

Success will not come to you; you must come to success. You can forfeit your chance for a happy, fulfilling life if you choose to shirk the responsibility of applying your best efforts and abilities to education. When you give only a minimum of effort to education, you receive only a minimum in return. Even when schools and teachers put forth their best efforts, in the end it is *your* work that determines how much and how well you learn.

Only when you take responsibility for your performance can you hope to learn skills that will enable you to create your future and control your destiny. You must decide to apply your talents and work with dedication and self-discipline. Only then can you begin your upward spiral of success.

Questions for Discussion

1. If things do not go well for you, will it change the results if you blame someone or something else? Explain your answer.

2. What is a loser's limp?

3. "Your success and your future are in your hands." Give some reasons why you agree or disagree with this statement.

4. "Success will not come to you; you must come to success." How should this statement influence your attitude as a student?

You have not lost until you start blaming someone else.
—John Wooden

You Usually Do Not Reach Someone Else's Goals

When you accept the responsibility for developing any new skill, it is absolutely necessary that you have the proper attitude. What is the proper attitude? It's believing that you *can* accomplish whatever you set out to accomplish. This positive attitude expresses itself in a cycle of forward momentum.

You believe. → You act. → You achieve. → You succeed.

If you want to improve your study habits, you must assume the attitude that you want to develop the best study skills possible. This is a decision only you can make. Without strong motivation on your part, nothing you do will make much difference. If someone else pressures or forces you to work on improving your study habits, you may start to do so, but your efforts will probably be short-lived. Remember, *you usually do not reach someone else's goals.* You must decide for yourself to improve your study habits and prepare to take action.

Somewhere along the line you may have picked up the idea that school is not relevant to your life today, that your efforts are just preparation for the future. Nothing could be further from the truth. Education *is* life, not merely preparation for it.

It's true that school and an education give you skills that will improve your chances for a successful future, but it's faulty reasoning to say, "I'm only going to school so that I will have a successful future." That won't work. It's much healthier to say, "I will develop my future success by learning how to be successful in school." Success is not a destination; it's a road on which you travel. As you travel the road of success, you discover more and more ways to be successful.

You can make success an ongoing attitude that will lead you down the road to greater successes. Learning to experience success in school and making success a part of your personality is as important as any skill you will learn. By learning how to succeed in school, you will learn how to succeed in life.

Successful students say, "I know where I am going, and I have the energy to get there." What is the reason for this self-assurance, for this positive attitude we all admire? The reason is success itself. Does that sound confusing? Let's analyze how the desire for success and achieving success can provide energy and drive to keep us going.

Most of us want to succeed. This desire is an energy source. That energy source helps us get up in the morning, get ready for school, attend class, study, and do the many other things that are required of us throughout the day. If that energy source is to keep providing power, however, we must recharge it from time to time. The best way to recharge it is to give it another shot of success.

Successes, even small successes, recharge our energy cells and keep them running at peak efficiency. When we feel the surge of elation from success, it gives us the drive to work harder. This ensures more success, and the upward spiral begins and accelerates.

Achieving success through learning leads directly to improving and maintaining a healthy self-image. Success in school fosters not only a sense of personal dignity and pride, but also a feeling of being in control. This positive self-image helps you develop a success-oriented personality.

Questions for Discussion

1.   "You usually do not reach someone else's goals." Discuss ways this statement applies to learning study skills.

2.   "Education is life, not merely preparation for it." Give reasons why you agree or disagree with this statement.

3.   How does the desire for success and achieving success provide you with an energy source?

4.   How does achieving success through learning lead directly to a healthy self-image?

> People often say that this or that person has not yet found himself. But the self is not something that one finds. It is something one creates.
> —Thomas Szasz

You Have Been Selected

Psychologists claim that many students use less than 40 percent of their mental capacity. Let's analyze what that means to you. Assume that you drive a six-cylinder car. If you were to disconnect three spark plug wires and if one of the three remaining spark plugs fired only about half the time, you would be using 40 percent of the car's total power. That would be a ridiculous waste of power and energy. It is also a waste of power and energy if you are not using all your mental power.

Some students may ask, "Why should I strive to be successful? Why work that hard? I'm pretty happy. I get by."

You must work hard to be successful because you are one of the chosen few. *You have been selected to be successsful.* There can be little doubt that this is so; just look around. More than 70 percent of the world's population has not been given the advantages that you have. Most of the people in the world do not live in houses that have plumbing and running water. Many families earn less than $360 per year. Many cannot afford to eat more than one meal a day. Many of the people in the world don't have even a third-grade education. You are one of the select few with a better education and with more comforts than most people in the world.

Along with your advantageous position comes an obligation: the obligation to try hard, to produce, and to excel. If you do not use your advantages, your intelligence, and your ability, you are not fulfilling your obligation to yourself and to society.

Please don't choose to wallow in mediocrity or failure.
Choose to be the best that you can be. Choose to use your ability
and your head start to become a leader. The fact that you have
chosen to improve your study skills indicates you have chosen
to take action to be a success. You are demonstrating that you are
determined to succeed.

Questions for Discussion

1. "You have been selected to be successful because you have
been given a head start on the rest of the world." What evidence
suggests that this statement is true?

2. Some people choose to wallow in mediocrity. They choose
to be less than they can be; they choose to waste their talents.
Discuss choices you can make that will help you to be the best
you can possibly be.

**People who try to do something and fail
are much better than those who try to do
nothing and succeed.**

—Lloyd James

Part 2

How to Manage Your Time

I wish I could stand on a busy street corner, hat in hand, and beg people to throw me their wasted hours.
—Bernard Berenson

You Cannot Manage Time

All of us have probably heard this advice: "The best way to take control of your life is to manage your time." You've heard it, haven't you? According to your teachers, "If you expect good grades, you must manage your time." And you've heard your parents say, "If you'd only learn to manage your time, you could get your work done and have time left to talk on the phone, too." It may sound like good advice, from people who care about you and have your best interests at heart. But these people have been giving you misleading advice—misleading because it can't be done. You cannot really "manage time." No one can. Why not?

You can *use* time, but you cannot *manage* it because you cannot control the hands on the clock. If you could manage time, you could cut 10 minutes off an hour if that hour happened to be boring. Or you could add 30 minutes to another hour if you needed more time to finish a test. Only if you had that magical ability to shorten and lengthen the hours could you ever hope to "manage time."

Since none of us has that magical ability, we must learn to manage *ourselves* as time passes. We must learn to manage ourselves each hour, each day, each week, each month, and each year. In managing ourselves, we can make the best possible use of our time. Only those students who learn to manage themselves efficiently can expect to find success.

Time is fleeting. It passes so quickly that there is really no such thing as "now." Think about it. When you try to pinpoint "now," it has already passed. "Now" melts away as soon as it arrives. For example, imagine the following conversation between an earthling and a creature from Mars. The Martian has just landed on earth and walks into a room where the earthling is working. A clock is hanging on the wall.

"Hello there," says the Martian. He points to the clock on the wall. "What's that?"

"Hello yourself," says the earthling suspiciously. "That thing you're pointing to is an instrument we use to measure time."

"How much time is it?" the Martian asks.

"It's 11:30," the earthling explains.

"I see," says the Martian. "It's 11:30. That's interesting."

"Well, it's not 11:30 anymore," says the earthling. "It's now 11:30 plus 10 seconds."

The Martian is confused. "You say it's 11:30, then you say it's 11:30 plus 10 seconds. Which am I to believe?"

"Well, neither," replies the earthling. "It's now 11:30 plus 20 seconds."

"Now see here!" shouts the Martian. "If that clock is going to tell you something different every time you look at it, why do you keep it hanging around?" Confused, he jumps into his spaceship and zooms back to Mars.

Time is a precious and vanishing item. When it passes so quickly, how can you ever expect to manage yourself so that you can use it before it vanishes?

The key to managing yourself efficiently within a certain period of time is to plan your activities. The best way to plan your activities is to make a time schedule. How do you prepare an effective time schedule? You must first understand and analyze how you are currently spending your time. After you understand exactly where your time has been going, you will be able to make better decisions about managing yourself.

Questions for Discussion

1. "You cannot manage time; you must learn to manage yourself as time passes." What is meant by that statement?

2. What is the key to managing yourself over a given period of time?

3. What must you do before you can prepare an effective time schedule?

> **The best way to ensure success is to do as well today as you expect to do tomorrow.**
> **—Anonymous**

You Needn't Be a Slave to the Clock

Students tend to be skeptical about the need for planning and scheduling their hours. Some feel it would be a waste of effort to make up an elaborate time schedule. Others feel that a schedule would tie them down and be too restrictive. On the contrary, efficient planning and scheduling can not only save you time, it can also increase your flexibility and provide you with more time to enjoy pleasurable activities.

As evidence of how this works, look at the way most people plan their vacations. Before they leave, they have usually planned the routes they are going to follow, where they are going to stay, and how much money they will spend. They plan very carefully because they want to get the most out of their precious vacation time. If planning allows us to get the most out of our two-week vacation, doesn't it make sense that we could get more out of the rest of the year if we also planned those weeks? Planning is the key to getting the most out of life during any time of the year.

Some students are afraid that a schedule will make them slaves to the clock. Just the opposite is true. Without a schedule you have very little flexibility. With no plan for how you will spend your time, it's easy to be disorganized, easy to procrastinate, easy to think "I have plenty of time to get that done," then wait too long to get started and not have time to do a good job. This disorganization and procrastination can affect both your grades and your personality. When you fall too far behind, you can easily adopt a defeatist attitude; you just give up. *With* a schedule, you are more in control of your time, and that gives you confidence.

People often complain, "I have so many things to do that I don't know which one to do first!" You've probably felt like this at times. In these situations, your indecision frequently causes such mental conflict that you delay getting started on any of the tasks. If you do manage to take action, you may jump frantically from one task to another, doing a half-hearted job on all of them. In order to be decisive and to free your mind to work toward your goals, you must learn to schedule and prioritize.

William James, a famous philosopher and psychologist, placed a great value on planning. He said, "The more details we can plan and schedule, the more the mind will be set free to concentrate on important work."

Planning and scheduling is well worth the effort. You will be in control. You will be in command of a less hectic, more efficient flow of events in your life. A schedule will allow you to enjoy your life more.

How Do You Use Your Time?

The first step in preparing a time schedule is to analyze how you are using your time now. Do you use it wisely or poorly?

One of the best ways to determine how well you're using your time is to chart what you do and how long it takes you to do it. Charting your time is simply recalling all the events of your day and writing them down in an orderly fashion so you can analyze where your time goes. Recalling the events of an entire day can be as difficult as trying to remember what happened to every penny of the ten dollars you spent last Saturday. The only way to keep an accurate account of either money spent or time used is to keep an itemized record.

A record of how you use your time is called a time diary. For this diary, you will use a *daily activity sheet* on which you list everything you did during the day and the amount of time you spent doing it. In some cases you will also want to indicate the particular people you spent time with, since, for example, time spent "talking" with your math teacher may be quite different from time spent "talking" with friends.

People are often surprised to learn how little they know about how they spend their time. One student speculated that he watched television about an hour and a half a day; he was surprised to learn that he actually watched it more than three hours a day. One teenager guessed that she was spending 30 minutes a day on snack breaks. In fact, her time diary told her that she was spending an average of 96 minutes a day snacking. You may find some surprises like these in your own time diary.

Researchers studying a group of 2500 students found that they spent their time in four main activities during a typical week: sleeping, attending class, studying, and eating. Of course, the students did other things as well, but these were the four primary activities. The following table shows a breakdown of the time the students spent in each activity.

Type of Activity	Hours Spent
Sleeping	49.3
In class	18.7
Studying	19.8
Eating	10.7
Total	98.5 hours

There are 168 hours in a seven-day week. When you subtract the 98.5 hours that are spent in the four main activities from 168 total hours, you are left with 69.5 hours. If you divide 69.5 hours by the seven days of the week, 10 hours a day are unaccounted for. Think about it—after you sleep, go to class, study, and eat your meals, there is an average of 10 hours each day to do everything else. Given this wealth of extra hours, you should be able to find enough time to do everything. But if you don't have time for everything, perhaps a time schedule will help.

Questions for Discussion

1.   Explain how a time schedule can help you be more decisive and keep your mind on your goals.

2.   Philosopher William James said, "The more details we can plan and schedule, the more the mind will be set free to concentrate on important work." Explain what he meant by this statement.

3.   What is a time diary?

4.   What is the first step in preparing a time schedule?

5.   Make a rough estimate of how many hours you spend each week sleeping, attending class, studying, and eating meals. Total them. Subtract that total from 168. The remainder will tell you how many hours a week you have left for other activities.

One of the rarest things a person ever does is the best he can.
                                                    —Josh Billings

Time Diary Exercise

   This exercise will help you begin to analyze how you use your time during a typical day and week. You will be asked to keep a complete record of your activities, day-by-day, for an entire week, using daily activity sheets and a weekly activity recap form.

   A completed daily activity sheet is shown on page 21. Study this example so you will understand how to log your time and activities. In the example, you will notice that all times are rounded to the nearest five minutes. It doesn't make much sense to be more exact than that. Even so, you should be careful to account, at least roughly, for every minute in a day.

Daily Activity Sheet

DATE: May 12

START	END	TIME USED	ACTIVITY DESCRIPTION
7:00	7:40	40 min.	woke up - shower - got dressed
7:40	8:05	25 min.	ate breakfast
8:05	8:30	25 min.	nothing
8:30	8:45	15 min.	walked to school
8:45	9:05	20 min.	talked to friends
9:05	9:55	50 min.	English class
9:55	10:00	5 min.	walking to class
10:00	10:50	50 min.	P.E. class
10:50	10:55	5 min.	walking to class
10:55	11:45	50 min.	math class
11:45	12:05	20 min.	lunch
12:05	12:30	25 min.	talked to friends
12:30	12:35	5 min.	walking to class
12:35	1:25	50 min.	History class
1:25	1:30	5 min.	walking to class
1:30	2:20	50 min.	Art class
2:20	2:25	5 min.	walking to class
2:25	3:15	50 min.	Typing class
3:15	3:35	20 min.	walked home
3:35	4:10	35 min.	listened to music - looked at magazines
4:10	4:25	15 min.	talked to Robert on phone
4:25	5:15	50 min.	math homework
5:15	5:40	25 min.	wrote book report
5:40	6:00	20 min.	read history assignment
6:00	6:40	40 min.	dinner with family
6:40	7:45	1 hr. 5 min.	played basketball at Jerry's house
7:45	10:00	2 hr. 15 min.	watched TV
10:00	10:30	30 min.	got ready for bed
10:30	7:00	8 hr. 30 min.	sleep

TIME SPENT ON ACTIVITIES

ACTIVITY	MONDAY		TUESDAY		WEDNESDAY		THURSDAY		FRIDAY		SATURDAY		SUNDAY		TOTALS	
	HOURS	MINS.	HOURS	MINS.	HOURS	MINS.	HOURS	MINS.	HOURS	MINS.	HOURS	MINS.	HOURS	MINS.	HOURS	MINS.
Classes	5	25	5	25	5	25	5	25	5	25		—		—	27	05
Studying	1	35	2	00	1	30	2	30		20		30	4	15	12	40
Eating	1	25	1	20	2	00	1	35	1	40	1	30	2	15	11	45
Sleeping	8	30	8	30	8	30	8	30	8	30	8	00	8	30	59	00
Going to and from school		35		35		40		30		45		30		—	3	35
Part-time job		—		—		—		—		—	6	00		—	6	00
Exercise	1	05	2	00	1	00	1	30		—	2	00	2	00	7	35
Television	2	15	1	05	1	30	1	00	2	00	4	00	4	00	15	50
Being with friends	1	00		30	1	00		15	3	15		30	1	00	7	30
Dressing/shower/etc.	1	10	1	30	1	20	1	00	1	15		45	1	00	7	00
Goofing off		35		45		20	1	30		30	2	15		40	7	35
Doing nothing		25		20		45		15		20		—		20	2	25

TOTAL FOR THE WEEK   168 00

Weekly Activity Recap

Instructions

1. Use lined paper to make seven daily activity sheets similar to the example on page 21. These sheets are the start of your own time diary. If possible, record your activities as you do them, rather than waiting until the end of the day and trying to remember what you did. This will make your diary more accurate.

2. Make a weekly activity recap form like the example shown on page 22. (You may want to make up your own general categories for the activities listed in the first column, but the ideas in the sample form should get you started.) When you have entered all your activities on this form, you will have a summary of how your time was spent over the entire week. This overview will help you find places you might make changes and improvements in your use of time.

When you have completed your daily activity sheets and the weekly activity recap, take time to carefully review this record. Notice if you spent too much time doing nothing. Perhaps you jumped from one task to another without getting much accomplished. There are no rules about how much time you should spend doing one thing or another; this is just a way of helping you see where the hours and minutes of your days really go, and where you might be able to make better use of them.

Making a Daily Plan

If you are faced with the problem of knowing that you must get more work done in a day's time, but you don't know how to go about it, perhaps the following true story will give you some ideas.

More than 50 years ago, Charles Schwab, the president of a small steel company, granted an interview to an efficiency expert named Ivy Lee. Mr. Lee said he could teach Mr. Schwab how to do a better job of managing his steel company. Mr. Schwab interrupted, saying, "I already know how to manage my company. I don't need more knowing. I need a lot more *doing*. We know what we should be doing, but if you'll show us an effective way of getting it done, I'll pay you anything within reason."

Mr. Lee responded, "I'll need just 30 minutes of your time to show you a way to get much more done and to make sure you're completing the most important tasks in their proper order." He handed Mr. Schwab a blank sheet of paper and instructed him to write down the six most important things he had to do the next day. It took Mr. Schwab about five minutes to make his list.

Mr. Lee then said, "Now, number the items on your list in order of their importance to you." Mr. Schwab took another five minutes to number his list.

Then Mr. Lee said, "Put that list in your pocket. First thing tomorrow morning, take it out and look at the first item. Don't look at the other items; just look at the first one and start working on it. Stay with it until you have completed it. Then take the second item and do the same thing; then the third, and so on, until the end of the day. Don't worry if you only finish two or three items that day. You'll be working on the most important ones. The others can wait. If you can't finish them all with this method, you couldn't have finished them all with any other method. And, without some system," Mr. Lee went on, "you'd probably take ten times as long to finish them and not even complete them in order of importance. Do this every day. After you're convinced of the value of this system, have your executives try it. Try it as long as you like, and then send me a check for whatever you think the idea is worth."

The entire interview took less than half an hour. In a few weeks, Mr. Schwab sent Ivy Lee a check for $25,000. He enclosed a note saying, "This is the most profitable idea I have ever used in my life!" Mr. Schwab later said that this simple idea was largely responsible for turning his small steel company into one of the biggest independent steel producers in the world: Bethlehem Steel.

The message for us is this: Take things one at a time, in their proper order, and stay with one task until it is completed before going on to the next. This idea made a great deal of difference to a steel company. Properly used, this idea can also make a big difference in your life.

Successful people make schedules. But successful people also *use* their schedules. The statement "Schedules don't work, people do" is true. It does little good to make an elaborate schedule of activities unless you also work at completing the items on that schedule.

A list of scheduled activities helps you plan how to get things done in order of their importance. While there will probably be occasions when you need to work on two or more tasks at the same time, a prioritized schedule can help you set aside the right amount of time for each task. Without a prioritized schedule, it's too easy to let "urgent" things interfere with "important" things. That is, suppose you are having a big math test on Friday. It's *urgent* that you study for this test, and maybe you're so concerned about it that you are tempted to spend all your study time reviewing your math.   But you also have a big 12-page research paper due the following Monday, and it's *important* that you keep working on it now rather than leaving it all for the weekend, because you can't do all the research and write the paper in just two days. With a prioritized schedule, you can set aside some time to work on the paper as well as study for the test. That way everything important gets done.

A simple schedule that you can refer to periodically throughout the day works best. For example, a three- by five-inch card will easily fit into your pocket or purse, or you could clip it to the front of a notebook that you take everywhere with you.

Sample Daily Schedule

Monday, October 8

7-8 Shower and breakfast
8-8:30 Review for history quiz
9-12:15 Classes
12:15-1 Lunch
1-3:15 Classes
3:15-4:30 Tennis with Michael
4:30-6 Dinner and goof-off
6-7:15 Complete math homework
7:15-8 Work on science project
8-8:30 Work on book report
8:30-10 Watch TV, relax, family time
10 To bed

It's best to prepare your schedule either the previous night or first thing in the morning. Take a few minutes to decide what you want to accomplish during the day and schedule the time needed for each task. In other words, simply jot down a plan for the day. Include classes you must attend, subjects you need to study, appointments, errands, exercise, recreation, "goof-off" time, and other activities. People find that making a schedule first thing in the morning gives them time to think through their day and start it with a sense of purpose. You might be surprised how effective this is.

The five or ten minutes you spend preparing a daily schedule are important for at least two reasons. First, you will have a list that you can refer to throughout the day. This will help unclutter your mind. Second, you will have thought through your day, setting your psychological time clock in motion.

Questions for Discussion

1.   Describe ways you can use Ivy Lee's method to help get your work completed on time.

2.   "Schedules don't work, people do." What does this statement mean?

3.   Explain this statement: "Without a prioritized schedule, it's easy to let *urgent* things interfere with *important* things."

4.   The five or ten minutes you spend preparing a time schedule helps get your day started with a purpose. It is also important for at least two other reasons. What are they?

Character consists of what you do on the third and fourth tries.
—James Michener

You Are the General Manager of Your Life

Learning to manage yourself is not a difficult task. You must simply analyze how you use your time and then decide on a plan that will make you more productive. A good plan will help you take charge of your life.

Here's one way to think of the task. Pretend your life is a business. Then visualize the different areas of your life as separate departments within the business. As the general manager of your business (your life), you are responsible for supervising all the departments. These separate departments must be carefully managed so they will function together effectively and smoothly.

What are some of these departments? There's the Coordinating Department. This department makes up your schedules, gets your tasks and assignments done on time, and generally keeps things running smoothly. Then there's the Income Department. This department's job is to earn money, keeping you supplied with cash.

Your business also includes a Human Relations Department to handle relationships between you and other people. It makes sure you are well-liked and respected by friends, teachers, and relatives. Your Purchasing Department is in charge of what you buy. It makes sure you do not spend more than you earn. You also have a Custodial Department that makes sure your body is clean and in good working order and keeps your clothes neat and attractive. As general manager, you are responsible for all these departments.

If your business is to function effectively, all the departments must perform their individual jobs. If one department lets the others down by not doing its job, the entire business (your life) suffers.

For example, suppose the Income Department drops the ball—it is not difficult to imagine what could happen next. If the Human Relations Department becomes rude and uncaring, there will certainly be problems. If the Coordinating Department adopts an "I don't care" attitude, you can be in big trouble—you could be late for class and your assignments may not get turned in on time. If the Purchasing Department does not keep an accurate accounting or mismanages your money, you may find yourself short of cash. If your Custodial Department gets sloppy and doesn't keep your clothes clean and neat, that may cause problems for the Human Relations Department.

All these departments are closely intertwined, but they are much easier to manage if you think of each one as a separate function. When a general manager in the business world finds the business in trouble, he or she usually takes a close look at the separate departments to see which ones are functioning smoothly and which ones are having difficulties. Those with problems are marked for changes. Handling the situation in this manner prevents the general manager from disrupting the entire business. Departments running smoothly are left to do their jobs while the manager concentrates on improving the departments that are having problems.

This same logic applies to you as the general manager of your life. If all the departments except the Coordinating Department are doing a good job, you need only concentrate on improving that department. When you improve the Coordinating Department, get to class on time, and keep up with your assignments, your entire life will improve. An analysis of your time diary will give you clues as to which departments in your life need improvement.

Concentrate on improving just one department at a time. With this approach the task of managing yourself will not seem so overwhelming.

Questions for Discussion

1. List some of the different departments that play important roles in *your* life.

2. Describe ways you can improve different departments so your business (your life) will function more effectively.

> **We learn courageous action by going forward when fear urges us back. A little boy was asked how he learned to skate. "Oh, by getting up every time I fell down," he answered.**
> —David Seabury

Goofing Off with Style and Effectiveness

When someone mentions "goofing off," students frequently react as though this were a bad word. It doesn't have to be. Goofing off is actually a good way to describe a very necessary lull in your hectic and stressful life.

Successful students budget their time so there is a balance between work, planned recreation, and good old-fashioned goof-off time. Without goof-off time, hardworking students suffer from fatigue and reduced performance.

Goof-off time, however, is only beneficial if it is worry-free. It does no good to goof off if you constantly worry about the things you should be doing, or if you feel guilty about taking time that you think you don't deserve.

If you worry and feel guilty when you goof off, you may start a vicious cycle. Stress from that worry and guilt may lead you to seek escape. Escape often takes the form of goofing off. More goofing off can cause even more worry and guilt feelings that lead you to seek further escape. It can be a depressing no-win cycle as you look for ways to escape from your obligations.

We let work slide, let it pile up until there seems to be no way to get it all done. When that happens, it's not uncommon just to want to take a nap and forget about everything. One sure way to prevent that frustrating feeling is to budget your time intelligently and set priorities. When you do this, it's easy to make a schedule that provides for goof-off time as well as for productive effort. An accurate time diary will provide the data you need to make a good, workable schedule. When you use the schedule intelligently, you will be effectively managing yourself and you will be destined for success.

Questions for Discussion

1. "Goof-off" is not necessarily a bad word. Why not?

2. How do successful and happy students budget their time?

> If a man insisted always on being serious, and never allowed himself a bit of fun and relaxation, he would go mad or become unstable without knowing it.
> —Herodotus

A Successful Life Starts with Successful Minutes

When confronted with an important task, some people make the mistake of viewing it as one big job instead of breaking it down into smaller, more manageable segments. Many young people make this mistake when they decide to become better students. With great resolve, they visualize themselves sitting for hours, grinding out page after page of homework. These lofty visions may seem promising, but they seldom work.

When you picture yourself studying for hours and hours, mastering the concepts of an entire textbook, you create a vision that is too big. It may be a worthy goal, but the rewards are too far in the future. You must wait too long to experience the gratification of a job well done.

Almost everyone will work hard toward something that will make them feel good. However, most of us lose interest if we have to wait too long for that happy result. This is particularly true if the work is not very exciting. To keep up your interest in studying, it is important to set easy-to-reach, short-term goals that you can feel good about accomplishing.

Instead of sitting down to study for three hours, most successful students have found it better to say to themselves, " In the next 15 minutes I am going to read and understand pages 352 and 353 of my textbook assignment." Then they note the time on the clock and begin to study. At the end of 15 minutes, they check their progress. Usually they have accomplished exactly what they set out to do. They set another goal for the next 15 minutes, then the next, and the next, until they have studied for three hours as originally planned.

You may want to try this. You will find that when you provide yourself with a series of gratifying experiences, each 15-minute period will instill the enthusiasm to carry on for another 15-minute period. After all, any of us can study effectively for just 15 minutes. Even A+ students, however, find it hard to concentrate with full effectiveness for three hours.

If you approach all of your studying in this manner, you will never again dread a ten-page reading assignment. You will never again feel overwhelmed by four hours of homework. You will deal with it in 15-minute periods, or one page at a time, until you are finished.

You may be thinking, "But I'll still have to read the entire ten pages. I'll still have to finish four hours of homework." Of course you will. Part of learning requires that you read your textbooks and complete your homework. But by approaching your work 15 minutes at a time, and experiencing the satisfaction of successfully completing those 15-minute periods, you are provided with a constant supply of "school fuel." School fuel is the energy created by successfully completing a task. It gives you enthusiasm and direction.

Students who master the art of being successful for only 15 minutes at a time have discovered the key to a successful way of life. After all, a successful hour is simply four successful 15-minute periods stacked together. A successful day is just a series of successful hours. A successful week is only seven successful days. A successful month is made up of just four successful weeks. A successful year is nothing more than a dozen successful months. And a successful life is just successful years joined together. So you see, a successful life begins by stacking just a few successful minutes together.

Questions for Discussion

1.   Why is it important for you to break a task down into manageable segments?

2.   What is "school fuel," and how can it help you maintain enthusiasm and direction?

3.   What is the key to a successful life?

> **Nothing is more depressing than to feel you missed the plum for lack of courage to shake the tree.**
> —Logan Pearsoll Smith

Go For It!

In the next chapters of this book you will learn four very important study skills:

- How to listen and take notes in class
- How to study your textbook
- How to study for tests
- How to take tests

When you learn these valuable skills, you will be prepared to achieve academic excellence.

You must keep in mind, however, that the mere possession of any skill will not guarantee success. Skilled swimmers will sink to the bottom of the pool if they do not use their skills to propel themselves forward. The same can be said of students who fail to use the study skills they have learned. Unless they use those study skills to propel themselves forward, they may be in danger of sinking to the bottom scholastically.

There is tremendous potential within you. When you apply yourself and learn to use sound study skills, you will experience the exhilaration of soaring to your full potential.

Go for it! Make a commitment to learn and to use sound study skills. Make a commitment to be the best student and the best person you can be.

The world stands aside to let anyone pass who knows where he is going.
                                                    —Jordan Allister

Part 3

How to Take Notes in Class

I will study, I will prepare, and my opportunity will come.
                              —Abraham Lincoln

Using Speed Writing

The first step in learning how to take notes in class is to practice some speed writing. Learning how to write faster is a skill that you will find invaluable for your studies. If you write faster, you can take more complete notes in class. And the better your notes, the better your grades—if you study your notes, of course!

The simplest form of speed writing to learn, and the most effective, is one you already know. You are probably thinking, "But I don't know how to do speed writing." Sure you do—you already know a form of speed writing that's based on common sense. Prove it to yourself with this exercise.

Exercise 1
Take out a sheet of paper and translate the following into words:

1. b	7. u	13. ne
2. 4	8. r	14. ᴜ̈
3. b4	9. u r	15. ᴧ̈
4. n	10. n4m	16. r u n
5. 2	11. 4ward	17. ndn
6. n2	12. c	18. ez

Now write this sentence using that same comon-sense form of speed writing:

19.   I see you before you see me.

See how easy that was? (If you want to check yourself, answers to the exercises in this section can be found in the Answer Key beginning on page 139.) You can probably think of many more words you could shorten this way, using letters and numbers or simple pictures.

Here's another speed writing idea that will help when you take notes. One of the most common sounds in the English language is the *th* sound. You hear the *th* sound in such words as *then, that, the, they, with,* and bo*th.* Instead of writing *th*, it's much faster to use a slash (/) for that sound. For example, you would write the word *they* like this: /*ey.* The word *this* would be written /*is.* The word *with* would be written *wi*/.

Exercise 2

Try substituting the slash for the *th* sound in the following words. Don't forget to use the first speed writing idea you have just learned. For example, *together* would be *2ge/er*.

1. they	**7.** therefore	**13.** brother
2. that	**8.** with	**14.** mother
3. then	**9.** both	**15.** rather
4. this	**10.** tooth	**16.** together
5. those	**11.** father	**17.** another
6. the	**12.** other	**18.** bother

Let's look at another idea that will help you write faster. The *ing* sound, as in go*ing*, do*ing*, and com*ing*, is the most common word ending in the English language. Therefore, we can write faster if we use a symbol that helps us write that word ending quickly. When you take notes, instead of writing *ing*, substitute a small circle (o) just above the line. Be careful not to use just a dot. A dot could be confused with a period.

If you use a small circle for the *ing* sound,
the word *going* would look like this: *go o*

The word *doing* would look like this: *do o*

Since you can use a slash for the *th* sound,
the word *thing* would look like this: */o*

The word *nothing* would look like this: *no/o*

Exercise 3

Use speed writing for the following words. Try substituting a small circle for the *ing* sound.

1. thing	**4.** nothing
2. something	**5.** things
3. everything	**6.** anything

Exercise 4
Now, using all the ideas you have learned to help you write faster, use speed writing for the following words.

1. going	**7.** learning	**13.** thing
2. doing	**8.** talking	**14.** something
3. wanting	**9.** jumping	**15.** informing
4. opening	**10.** eating	**16.** seeing
5. running	**11.** thinking	**17.** being
6. walking	**12.** nothing	**18.** are you in

You now have the basic skills for writing faster. As you see, you don't need to learn a fancy shorthand system; you simply use in a slightly different way things you already know. If you take these basic ideas and think creatively, you will undoubtedly find ways to use speed writing with many different words and phrases. You may even devise your own personal shortcuts for common words, common word endings, or names that come up again and again as you take class notes. For example, once you have written *Shakespeare* the first time during an English lecture, you may simply refer to him as *S* in the rest of your notes on that lecture. Anything goes—as long as you can read it all later when you go back to study your notes.

Exercise 5
Write the following words, using what you've learned about speed writing.

1. be	**7.** in	**13.** any
2. became	**8.** invented	**14.** with
3. for, fore	**9.** increase	**15.** earth
4. before	**10.** than	**16.** easy
5. to, too	**11.** there	**17.** because
6. together	**12.** believe	**18.** they are in

Exercise 6
Translate the following into words.

1. /ey	8. bo/	15. ano/er	22. n4m₀
2. /at	9. fa/er	16. 2/	23. c₀
3. /em	10. o/er	17. some/₀	24. bo
4. /is	11. bro/er	18. every/₀	25. walk₀
5. /ose	12. mo/er	19. no/₀	26. eat₀
6. /e	13. ra/er	20. /₀s	27. want₀
7. wi/	14. 2ge/er	21. ne/₀	28. /ink₀

Great minds have purposes, others have wishes.
—Washington Irving

Common Questions and Misconceptions About Note Taking

While your science teacher is describing the structure of certain molecules, or your history teacher is explaining what led to World War I, do you write down the important points being made? You may not think it's necessary. Many students question if it is worth the time and effort to take notes. They share some common misconceptions about note taking. Let's examine a few of their questions and misconceptions.

Why should I take notes? I seem to remember just as much if I listen carefully.

Most students understand that a textbook chapter is to be read, outlined, and studied when it is assigned. Later, before an exam, they know they must study it again. Unfortunately, many students think that if they listen to what the teacher says in class and understand it, they don't need to devote any further study to that classtime material. Don't make that mistake!

Studies have shown that when students do not take notes in class, they often forget within 15 minutes *almost half* of what the teacher said. Even worse, after 24 hours many students will have forgotten more than 60 percent of what the teacher said, and after two weeks they will have forgotten more than 80 percent. This occurs when students do not take notes in class and review those notes at least once a week.

Your class notes should be viewed as a book that you wrote yourself. You need to study this handwritten book just as you study your textbooks. Keep in mind that many teachers would rather test you on the ideas they present in class than on the ideas presented in the book.

Another important fact to keep in mind is that good teachers talk in class about 80 percent of the time. If your teacher talks 80 percent of the time and you forget half of what he or she says within 15 minutes, you will be forgetting important information. Your grades will suffer. To be the best student you can be, you *must* learn to take notes in class.

Wouldn't it be better to use a tape recorder so I can be sure to get all the information?

The answer to that question is an emphatic NO! It may sound like a good idea, but if you tape-record a 50-minute lecture, how can you review it without listening to the entire 50 minutes of tape? Taping each class period can easily *double* the time you must spend studying. Research conducted by the Study Skills Institute of California found that fewer than 7 percent of the students who taped lectures ever listened to the tape again.

You attend class so you can listen to the teacher and write down the most important points. Learning to take good notes helps you do this. Listening to a lecture twice is not an efficient use of your valuable time. Furthermore, taping a lecture often lulls you into being inattentive and daydreaming during class—you think you don't need to listen because you will have it all on tape. It just doesn't work.

Won't note taking interfere with listening?

Absolutely not. A study demonstrated that students who take notes in class score higher on tests given immediately after a lecture than students who do not take notes. In this study, lecture notes were collected immediately after the lecture so students did not have time to study them.

The same study also revealed that students' long-term remembering was markedly improved when they took notes, *even if they did not study those notes later*. Further studies demonstrated that students who take notes and study them just once a week can recall as much as 90 percent more of a lecture after six weeks than students who do not take notes. As you can see, note taking does *not* interfere with listening; in fact, if the test scores are any indication, note taking helps students listen and concentrate in class.

My teacher wants us to use three-ring binders and loose-leaf notebook paper. Isn't it better to use a spiral-bound notebook, so the pages won't get lost?

A three-ring binder is the best choice because it allows you more flexibility in organizing your notes. When you use a three-ring binder, write only on the front side of the paper as you take notes. This leaves room on the back of the paper for you to jot down additional notes when you study and gather more information from your textbook. A three-ring binder also enables you to insert hand-outs and assignment sheets in their proper order. A study conducted by the Study Skills Institute discovered that students who took notes in a three-ring binder had better-organized notes, with more information and more support materials, than students who used other types of notebooks.

Is it a good idea to retype my notes later?

Some students believe that retyping or copying their notes is a good way of studying. That is not necessarily true. Most people find it difficult to concentrate fully on two activities, such as typing and studying, at the same time. Students generally find that typing requires their full concentration, and studying also needs their undivided attention. Most students cannot do both properly at the same time. Taking good notes in class makes retyping and copying them unnecessary.

Can I write down just the main ideas? Will that be enough?

No, writing just the main ideas will not give you the thorough information you need to study your notes. Main ideas and general statements are of little use without sub-ideas, details, and examples that provide supporting evidence. You should always try to come out of class with enough information to form a complete concept.

Also keep in mind that during a lecture, you should not stop and reflect on the material while the teacher is talking. If you stop to dwell on an idea too long, chances are great that when your mind goes back to the lecture you will have missed some important points. (Of course, this is not true if the class is spent in discussion instead of a lecture. During discussion, you *do* need to be thinking about the material, not just taking notes. Otherwise you'll have nothing to contribute.)

When the teacher talks too fast, how can I keep up?

When you are faced with this problem (and it occurs quite often), use a two-page system in your three-ring binder. On the left-hand page, record only the main ideas in a bold, abbreviated way. Make sure you write down all the key words. During lulls in the lecture, or immediately after the lecture, record as many details as you can on the right-hand page opposite the main ideas and key words. You will then have an easy-to-review lecture in outline form on the left with a full page of supporting details on the right.

Shouldn't I wait until after a lecture to read the textbook chapter?

That's not a good idea. Often a teacher's classroom lecture will follow the topics in the order they appear in the textbook. By reading your textbook before the lecture you will already be familiar with the material. This way you can anticipate important points and easily follow the development of the topic.

You may not have many teachers right now who spend the whole class period lecturing, but some day you may—especially if you plan to go to college. If you learn how to take good notes now, you'll be prepared for that day.

Questions for Discussion

1.   Suppose one of your friends says, "I don't need to take notes, I think I remember just as much if I only listen in class." What would you say to convince your friend to take notes?

2.   Within how many minutes will many students forget almost half of what a teacher said in class?

3.   Is it a good idea to use a tape recorder in class instead of relying on your notes? Why or why not?

4.   Will note taking interfere with listening to a lecture? Explain your answer.

5.   Should you take notes on unbound paper, in a spiral notebook, or in a three-ring binder? Explain your answer.

6.   Is it a good idea to retype your notes? Why or why not?

7.   Is it enough to write down only the main ideas in class? Explain your answer.

8.   Is it a good idea to wait until after a lecture to read the textbook chapter? Why or why not?

9.   When your teacher talks too fast, what method can you use to take good notes?

A problem is a chance to do your best.
—Duke Ellington

Don't Give Your Mind Excused Absences from Class

Most serious students agree that skipping class will result in less learning and, therefore, have an adverse effect on grades. Yet almost all students "cut class" from time to time without even being aware of it—and they do it inside the classroom.

How can you cut class when you're sitting in the classroom? By letting your mind wander, letting it go someplace else. When you daydream or think about something besides the lecture, only your body is in the classroom. Your body is mindless. When your body is mindless, it becomes fidgety and uncomfortable. It gets bored because your mind is not there to tell it what to do.

Cutting class inside the classroom can do more damage than being physically absent from class. Most students who are physically absent understand that they have to make up the work they missed. But students who cut class inside the classroom believe they are keeping up when, in fact, they are not.

Don't give your mind excused absences from class. You are making a commitment to your education by attending class. Follow through on your commitment by paying attention to the lecture. Your commitment will require some self-discipline, but it will reward you with heightened interest and better grades.

Questions for Discussion

1. How can you sit in your seat in the classroom and still be absent from class?

2. Why does cutting class inside the classroom often have a more serious effect on your grades than actually skipping class?

3. What can happen if your body is *mindless* in class?

4. Why should self-discipline in class be important to you?

> **Do not neglect the gift that is in you.**
> **—1 Timothy 4:14**

The Computer Every Student Can Use

Wouldn't it be great if you had a computer-like device you could take to class with you that would receive, record, and catalog all the information presented in class? Once the information was received and cataloged, you could get an instant readout on that information by simply punching a memory key.

As with most computer-like devices, this one would have to be properly programmed to receive, record, and catalog information. But if it were properly programmed and turned on, it could work wonders for you.

Do you wish you had one of these fantastic devices? You do! This computer-like device is your brain. Your brain is the most fantastic tool you have. Your brain can do almost unbelievable things. All you have to do is properly program it.

The following section of this book will show you how to program your fantastic computer-like device to receive, record, and catalog everything you hear in class. Then, when you activate your memory key, you will get a complete and accurate readout. Just transfer this information to your test paper, and your performance in school will soar.

As you program your computer-like device, you need to be aware that it can sometimes short-circuit and malfunction. How do you cause a short circuit? One of the quickest ways is to try to memorize too many things. Your brain will remember thousands of things if you let it work naturally. But when you require a lot of memorization, it may rebel, short-circuit, and malfunction. In this section you will learn how to avoid this by using a memory key to retrieve the information you want.

Let's explore what is meant by the term *memory key*. How many times in the last few days have you heard, thought, or seen something that caused you to snap your fingers and say, "Oh yes, that reminds me . . ."? Of course it has happened to you; it has happened many times to all of us. In effect, whatever you heard, thought, or saw was a memory key. When that memory key was punched, it began to give you a readout on the data stored in the memory cells of your brain.

Another example illustrates this idea further. Suppose you were talking about the discovery of America, and someone said, "In 1492 . . ." What would come to mind? If you're like many of us, you would probably think, "In 1492, Columbus sailed the ocean blue." When you punched the "1492" memory key, you began to get a readout that included information about Columbus, the *Niña*, the *Pinta*, the *Santa María*, Queen Isabella, King Ferdinand, the New World, and probably much more. One small memory key caused your computer-like brain to start processing the required data and to produce a wealth of information.

This memory-key method for recalling information is not really new. In fact, it is remarkably similar to an ancient method that has been used for centuries. Let's see how that ancient method worked.

The Ancient Method of Remembering

Centuries ago, when there was no written word, the ability to *remember* historical events, birth dates, songs, legends, and even who was related to whom was extremely important. Because people had no written record of events and facts, the information was passed by word of mouth from one generation to another as oral history.

It was not unusual for the wise old people of a tribe to be able to recite history and legends that went back many generations. These historical recitations often lasted several days. Even though this feat required an almost unbelievably good memory, they seldom left out any details.

How were these ancient people able to remember so many things? Did they have a better memory than ours today? Of course not. They could remember all those things because they had a method for remembering. The method that was used so effectively hundreds of years ago by tribal historians is today called *association*.

The tribal historian did not try to memorize the many events of the tribe's history. Instead, he associated each historical event with some part of a familiar journey. When the historian took that familiar journey in his mind, each part of the journey reminded him of something that had happened to his tribe. For example, suppose the journey led him first up a path thick with thorny bushes and jagged rocks. That might remind the historian of a battle with an enemy tribe. Thinking about the thorns and jagged rocks that tore at his clothes and punctured his skin would bring to mind the wounds of battle. The next part of the journey might lead him across a river. The water in the river would remind him of the year of the great floods.

Each part of that familiar journey, then, was a memory key. As the historian mentally took the journey, each memory key was triggered in turn, giving him a readout on what he wanted to remember.

In the following pages, we will explore ways to use this method of association to provide memory keys for your class notes. These memory keys will enable you to easily recall almost all the information presented during a lecture.

Questions for Discussion

1. How is your brain like a computer that you can take to class with you?

2. It was not unusual for wise historians of ancient tribes to recite history and legends that went back many generations. How were these ancient historians able to accomplish this?

3. How could you use association or memory keys to help you remember material you want to learn?

> **There is no security on earth; there is only opportunity.**
> **—Douglas MacArthur**

The Memory-Key Method

There are four steps in the memory-key method for taking notes. Each step is very important and should be followed every time you take notes in class.

Step 1: Get Ready to Take Notes

To get ready, draw a vertical line down the left side of several sheets of notebook paper. The line should be about two and one-half inches from the left edge (see figure 1). This line divides your notepaper into two parts. You will use the part to the *right* of the vertical line to write down your class notes. You will use the part to the *left* of the vertical line to write down your memory keys. You might say that the space to the right of the line is your *memory bank* and the space to the left is your *memory keyboard*.

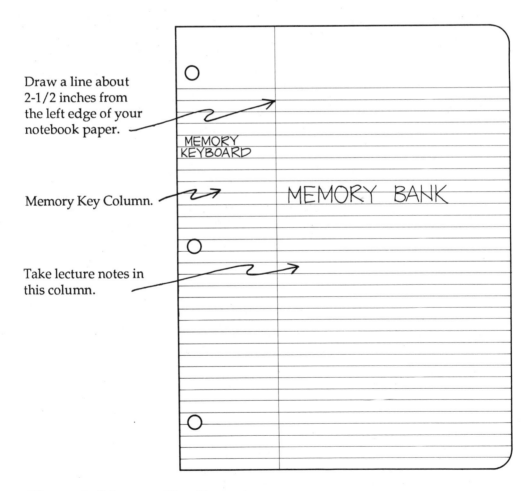

Figure 1. Memory Key Format.

Step 2: Take Notes

During class, follow these rules as you take notes:

- Record your notes in simple paragraph form on the memory bank side of your notepaper. Do not try to set up elaborate outlines with Roman numerals, capital letters, and lower case letters. Just write down the facts and ideas as you hear them. Make sure you put down enough information so your notes will have meaning to you when you study them.

- Skip lines between different points and ideas.

- Write fast, using speed writing and abbreviations whenever possible. Be sure to write legibly and avoid abbreviations and phrases that will be difficult to decipher. Sloppy notes will mean that later you have to spend time deciphering instead of studying. Keep in mind, however, that incomplete sentences are perfectly good form when you're taking notes.

Step 3: Clarify Your Notes and Add Memory Keys

As soon as possible after class, go through your notes to clarify your thoughts and to make scribbled words easier to read. This will help to reduce the amount of information you forget.

In the memory column, write important words and phrases or draw simple stick-figure pictures. These will be your memory keys. As you select memory keys, you will be forced to review all the ideas presented in class and to think about them in your own words. This kind of review is an excellent way to improve your long-term memory.

It is very important that you do not attempt to add memory keys while the teacher is explaining subject material. If you concentrate on selecting memory keys while your teacher is talking, you are likely to miss important information. But if your teacher stops lecturing occasionally during class, you can use this time to add your memory keys.

Step 4: Study Your Notes

Once you've taken notes, it's important to review them periodically. At your first opportunity, cover up the right side of your notes (your memory bank) with a sheet of paper. Using only the memory keys, recite *out loud* the facts and information presented in class. Then uncover your notes and see how well you recalled the material you wrote in the memory bank. This form of studying your notes is the most powerful learning method you can use. It combines seeing, hearing, and doing— the three basic channels of learning.

Studying your memory keys once a week will help you retain the information. You needn't spend a long time studying; just review what you've learned so far. This will help make studying for a test much easier.

These four simple steps are the keys to good class notes. When you become adept at these procedures, you will find that you remember almost all the material presented in class.

Questions for Discussion

1. What is step 1 of the memory-key method for taking notes?

2. When you have completed step 1, your notepaper is divided into two parts. Describe the purpose of each part.

3. What is step 2 of the memory-key method? What are the rules for this step?

4. Name and describe step 3 of the memory-key method. When is the best time to do this step?

5. What is step 4 of the memory-key method? How and when do you do step 4?

I find that a great part of the information that I have was acquired by looking up something and finding something else along the way.

—Franklin Adams

Don't Write Down Everything That's Said

When you take notes in class, your goal is to write as many meaningful facts and ideas as you can in the memory bank of your notepaper. The most important word in the previous sentence is *meaningful*. Most teachers know that if they stand in front of a class and simply recite facts and figures, their students will be sound asleep in a few minutes. In order to prevent boredom and keep students from nodding, they use colorful, descriptive language. Usually this colorful language and descriptive phrasing does not need to be written down in your notes because it is not meaningful to the subject.

Consider the following excerpt from a physical science lecture (you'll find the complete lecture later in this section):

Everyone loves a mystery. It might be a fictional one, such as "Who stabbed the millionaire while he was sipping brandy in his study when all the windows and doors were locked from the inside?" Or it might be a historical one, such as "Did Amelia Earhart's plane really crash, or is she possibly still alive?"

There are also mysteries of science, mysteries that are far broader in scope and much more important to mankind. In science, just as in police stories, there are detectives who gather clues—clues that are much harder to trace than a fingerprint left at the scene of the crime.

One of the great scientific mysteries of today is earthquakes. In ancient times, many people believed earthquakes were caused by angry gods to punish mankind.

Most of this lecture segment is colorful and descriptive. The references to the millionaire and to Amelia Earhart are designed to catch your attention as the speaker leads into the subject of earthquakes as mysteries of science.

Teachers are not likely to ask questions about either the millionaire or Amelia Earhart on a test about earthquakes. Therefore, in your notes you need cover only these facts:

- Earthquakes are mysteries of science.
- Ancient people believed earthquakes were caused by angry gods to punish mankind.

Your notes from this portion of the lecture might look like the sample shown in figure 2. Later, you would add a memory key on the left—maybe "ancient beliefs." (You'll learn about selecting good memory keys in the next few pages.)

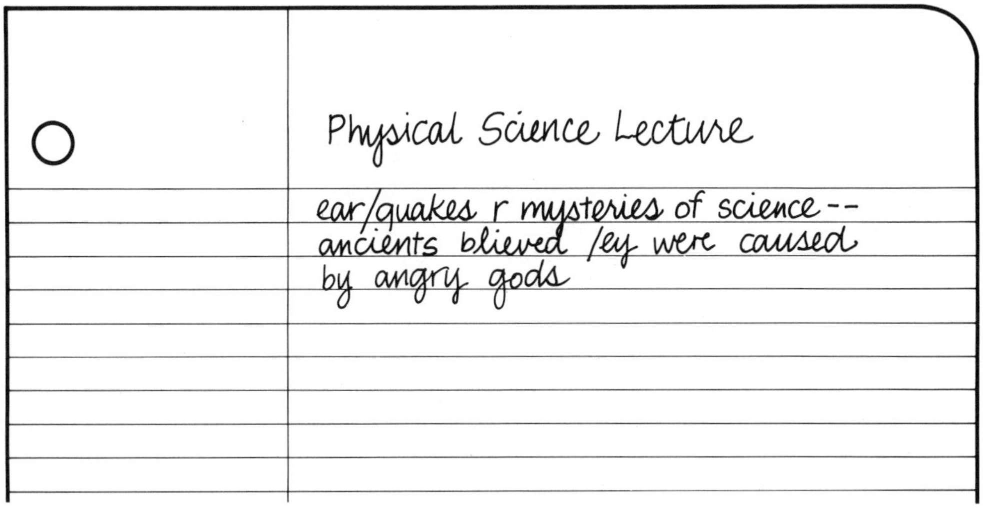

Figure 2. Class notes for lecture excerpt.

Now let's consider another part of the same lecture:

When will the next great earthquake come? If it cannot be stopped, will we have enough warning to get everyone to safety before it happens?

The knowledge about earthquakes gathered in recent years has been tremendous, but it still isn't enough to let us know when one of the earth's plates will scrape against another and set the earth trembling. Most of the time the plates are wedged tightly against each other and held motionless. However, the strain slowly increases from year to year. Eventually, some slight nudge will set off a tremor that may cause another big earthquake. What will cause that nudge? Where will it come from? And when?

Doctors John Gribbon and Stephen Plaggeman are searching for clues on when that nudge will occur.

This segment of the lecture, like the first segment, has a lot of conversational material designed to hold your attention. Much of it does not need to be written in your notes. Your notes and memory keys for the lecture to this point might look something like figure 3.

	Physical Science Lecture
Ancient beliefs	ear/quakes r mysteries of science -- ancients blieved /ey were caused by angry gods
Gribbon & Plaggeman	plates usually wedged 2ge/er. still can't predict when ear/'s plates will move. Dr.s Gribbon & Plaggeman search. 4 clus

Figure 3.   Class notes with memory keys added.

Selecting Memory Keys

When you select memory keys, you can use anything that will trigger your brain to recall associated facts, ideas, or figures. As your skill in using the memory-key method improves, the best key words or phrases will become increasingly obvious to you. In the meantime, while you are still developing this skill, the hints listed below can help you select good memory keys.

Hints for Selecting Memory Keys

1.   Memory keys should be as short as possible. A single word, or a three- or four-word phrase at most, is enough. A simple sketch or stick figure can also be an excellent memory key.

2.   If you have difficulty remembering a term, name, fact, or figure from a lecture, make that your memory key.

3.   Use dates as memory keys. Most students have trouble remembering dates. If you use the date as a memory key, your mind will automatically associate the date with the event you need to remember. It's an easy way to remember those pesky dates.

4. When you select a memory key, form a vivid mental picture of that key. Medical researchers have found that an electrical impulse flashes to the vision center of your brain when you look at an object. These researchers also discovered that the same electrical impulse could be activated by forming a vivid mental picture. When this electrical impulse is very strong, it aids long-term memory. Forming a vivid mental picture of your memory key is very important.

5. Always select *your own* memory keys. Memory keys are associations, and your associations are as personal, unique, and individual as your own fingerprints. If you borrow someone else's memory keys, they may not be associated with anything in your memory bank. It is extremely important to select memory keys that work for *you*.

6. You may change your memory keys later if necessary. If you find that a particular memory key does not trigger a quick response from your memory bank, change it. Find one that works. There is nothing wrong with changing this part of your notes.

7. Remember not to add memory keys while your teacher is still talking about the subject material. Instead, concentrate on listening and taking notes while the teacher is talking. Add your memory keys only when the teacher pauses or after class.

Memory Key Examples

Let's explore some different kinds of memory keys you might use for a class lecture. Suppose your teacher is talking about whales. The teacher might say, "Whales must come to the surface of the ocean in order to breathe. When they come to the surface, they spout. A spout is actually air being expelled from a whale's lungs. The air is expelled through a *blow hole* on the whale's back."

In your notes, you might write:

Whales surface 2 breale. Spout /ru blow hole.

For that idea, some possible memory keys might be:

spout  blow hole

Your teacher continues the lecture by saying, "After whales surface and spout, they dive again beneath the surface. When whales dive beneath the surface, it's called *sounding*."

You jot down in your notes:

whales dive - called sound.

For your memory key, you might sketch a picture of a whale's tail or use the words *whale's tail* because the tail is the last thing you see when a whale sounds. Any of these could be good choices:

sounding diving

With memory keys added, then, your notes for the beginning of the whale lecture might look like the example in figure 4. (Keep in mind that they wouldn't *have* to look like this. These are just ideas to show you what's possible.)

O	*whales*
	whales surface 2 break. Spout /ru *blow hole*
	whales dive - called sound.

Figure 4.   Class notes with memory keys added.

Now you try it. See what memory keys you can devise for the material you've been learning in this section.

Instructions

1. Prepare a sheet of notepaper in the memory key format by drawing a line two and one-half inches from the left edge.

2. In the memory bank side of your notepaper, write information from each one of the seven "Hints for Selecting Memory Keys" (beginning on page 54). Do not write the entire hint, but just enough notes to show that you understand the hint.

3. After you have entered information in the memory bank for all seven hints, add memory keys in the keyboard side of your notepaper.

For example, your notes and memory key for the first hint might look like figure 5.

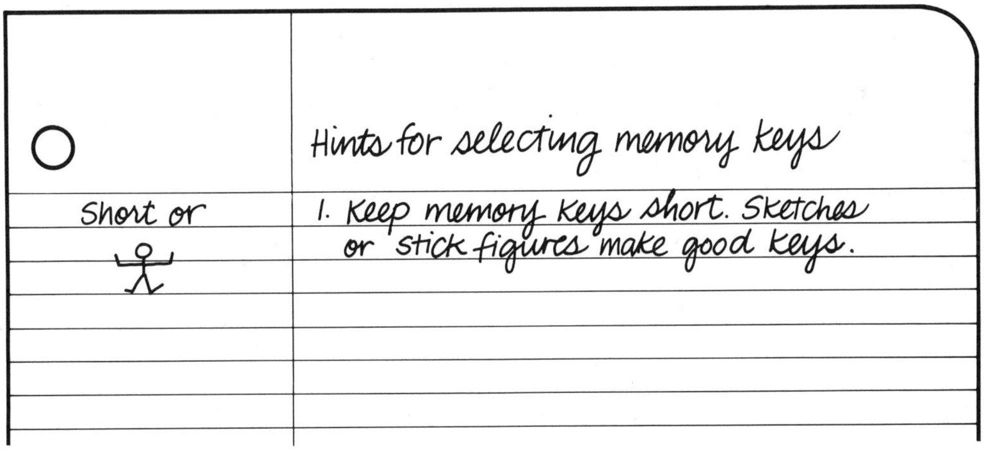

Figure 5. Possible notes and memory key for the first hint.

When you have finished, cover your memory bank with a sheet of paper. Using only your memory keys, can you name all seven hints? If not, change your keys to make them better. Then try again.

That's all there is to the memory-key method. It's simple, and it works. Make it work for you.

Memory Key Practice Exercises

Here are four short mini-lectures to give you a chance to practice taking notes and devising memory keys. The more you practice this method, the easier it will be when you are actually sitting in class listening to a teacher.

Instructions

1.   Prepare several sheets of paper in the memory-key format.

2.   Read each of the following lectures. As you read, pretend you are in class listening to a teacher and take notes on the material that's being presented. Remember, do *not* write anything in the memory key column until after the lecture is over.

3.   When you have finished taking notes on one lecture, add your memory keys.

4.   Cover your notes and, using only the memory keys, see how much of the information you can remember.

5.   Follow the same procedure for each lecture that follows.

If you like, compare your work with the sample pages of notes and memory keys in the Answer Key on pages 141-44. Of course there are no right or wrong answers; what's important is that your notes and memory keys work for you.

Lecture 1
Facts About the Moon

The moon may appear large to us, but it is actually not as large as the sun or the stars. The moon just *looks* larger because it is closer to the earth than either the sun or the stars are.

The moon is about 200,000 miles from the earth. It takes a spaceship almost 64 hours to reach the moon.

On the moon, days and nights each last about two weeks. It gets very hot during the day and very cold during the night. This is because there is no air on the moon. Because there is no air, there are no plants or animals.

The moon's surface gravity is only one-sixth the surface gravity of the earth. Because there is so little gravity, if you weighed 120 pounds on earth, you would weigh only one-sixth of that, or 20 pounds, on the moon.

Lecture 2
Christopher Columbus

Christopher Columbus was born in Genoa, Italy about 500 years ago. He was an excellent sailor and eventually became a famous explorer. Some people who lived in his time believed the world was flat. Columbus was convinced the world was round. He also thought the world was much smaller than it actually is.

Columbus wanted to sail to India, which he knew was east of Italy. Because he thought the world was round, he believed he could reach India in a shorter time by sailing west. Columbus went to the kings of Portugal and England seeking help and permission to sail, but they both refused. Columbus did not give up, however. For seven years he tried to get permission from King Ferdinand and Queen Isabella of Spain. Finally, they consented and gave him men and ships.

Columbus never reached India, but in 1492 he reached a large body of land now called America.

Lecture 3
The Dragonfly

A dragonfly is a very interesting insect. It has two pairs of large wings and a long slender body. These features make the dragonfly look like a tiny airplane. The dragonfly's eyes are actually made up of many small eyes that allow it to see in almost every direction at once.

Dragonflies live around swamps and in still water where they can find insects to eat, such as mosquitoes. The fact that dragonflies eat mostly mosquitoes makes them very valuable to man.

The female dragonfly lays her eggs on the water's surface or on plants in the water. These eggs usually hatch in about two weeks. The small dragonflies live in the water from one to five years before becoming adults. During this time their skin will change several times.

Lecture 4
Listening and Hearing

The ear is a truly marvelous organ of the human body. Ears enable us to hear all kinds of sounds. People talking, music, the call of a bird—these are just a few. You might think that *hearing* and *listening* mean the same thing, but that's not entirely true. We can *hear* something, but it may not mean anything to us unless we are *listening* as well. When we listen, we hear sounds that mean something to us. We hear with our ears; we listen not only with our ears, but also with our minds and our feelings.

Listening involves four things: attention, hearing, understanding, and remembering. If your teacher wants you to do something, the teacher must first get your attention. The sounds the teacher makes, in the form of words, must fall on your ears so you hear them. As you hear the words, you must interpret them so you can understand their meaning. Then you must remember what the teacher said so you can follow directions.

Have you ever heard the sayings, "What goes in one ear comes out the other" and "I might as well be talking to a stone wall"? These are just other ways of saying that people may *hear* you without listening to you. They do not listen to the meaning of the words. If you were about to cross a busy street and a car horn sounded, what would you do? If you simply *heard* the horn, you might walk right out in front of the car. But if you *listened* to the horn, you would interpret it as a warning and remain on the sidewalk until the car passed. The same principle applies to speech. We often hear the words, but unless we listen carefully, we are like the stone wall in the saying.

Practice for Taking Notes in Class

Here's a chance to practice note taking with some longer lectures. For this exercise, pretend that a series of guest speakers will be coming to speak to your class. The teacher wants you to take notes, as you will be discussing the speeches in class later.

For the best practice, have someone read the following three lectures to you as you take notes. If this is not possible, simply pretend you are listening to the guest speakers as you read the lectures yourself. Take notes, then add memory keys in the left column of your notepaper.

Remember: Do not add memory keys until *after* you have finished taking notes on each lecture.

Guest Lecture 1
Believe in Yourself

The dictionary defines *handicap* as "(noun) something that hampers a person; a disadvantage; (verb) to hinder."

Is this definition always true? What are some widely known handicaps? Blindness, paralysis, loss of an arm or leg, and brain disorders are just a few of the most common handicaps.

If you had one of these handicaps you might think it was the end of the world. For example, if you were blind, think of all the things you could not see—your clothes, your food, your friends, your family, yourself. You would have a difficult time getting around in a strange place if there was no one to guide you. You might think that there would be very little you could do.

Think again. Other senses would become sharper if you were blind. Your nose would detect odors you had not noticed before. Blind people often smell the smoke of a fire long before others smell it. Their early warnings have saved lives and property.

Have you ever noticed that blind people touch objects and people much more than most of us do? They must use their sense of touch in place of their eyes. Their fingers are often much more sensitive than a seeing person's fingers. For example, they use their fingers to read. Louis Braille, a Frenchman, invented Braille in the 1800s to make it possible for blind people to read and write. With his invention, the blind had a way to communicate on paper, using their fingers as "eyes."

The sense of hearing is also more sensitive for blind people. Their ears hear subtleties that most of us miss. For example, many of us are not always aware of the tone of voice we use. Many blind people are better than sighted people at hearing differences in tone of voice that convey fear, happiness, sadness, and other emotions. Many can also pick up music by ear—playing without reading musical notes. There are many excellent blind musicians; Stevie Wonder, José Feliciano, Ronnie Milsap, and Ray Charles are just a few.

When Ray Charles was five years old, he began to lose his sight. His parents didn't have enough money to take him to an eye specialist, so the doctor in his hometown did what he could. He prescribed eye drops, but they did no good. By the time he was seven years old, Ray Charles was blind. Doctors now tell him that he must have had glaucoma.

Sometimes it takes a long time for blind children to adjust to a world of darkness. Not Ray Charles. Ray's mother was the main reason he adjusted so quickly. She refused to let him sit and do nothing. "You're blind, not stupid. You've lost your eyes, not your mind," she told him.

She taught Ray how to deal with his blindness by forcing him to do many things such as scrub floors, chop wood, and other chores. She told him he would have to learn to do things for himself because someone would not always be around to help him.

Ray learned Braille in the State School for the Blind in Florida. He also studied music at the school.

When Ray was 15 years old, his mother died. After she died, he lived with friends. Finally he remembered what his mother had taught him about being independent. He went out on his own and traveled by himself to Orlando, Florida. There he joined a band. The band was not very good and eventually broke up, but Ray refused to admit defeat. He traveled to Seattle, Washington, where he was hired by a nightclub.

Ray Charles eventually achieved success. He became one of the most famous musicians the world has ever known. Even though he lost his sight, he didn't give up. He believed in himself and in his ability. That lesson should be very important to everyone.

Kitty O'Neal said it best. Kitty, a stunt woman who holds many land and water speed records, is also deaf. She said, "Handicapped is a word. It's not a way of life."

All of us have some kind of problem to overcome. It might be a problem understanding math or English or history. It doesn't matter what our problem may be; to each of us it's very important. Just remember: You can overcome that problem if you believe in yourself and in your ability to succeed.

Guest Lecture 2
Self-Image—The Strongest Force Within You

It is a proven fact that you act and feel according to the image your mind holds of what things *seem like*, instead of according to what things *are really like*. You behave as if those images were true regardless of whether they in fact are.

For example, picture this scene: The night after you have seen the movie *Jaws*, you are swimming in the ocean at your favorite beach. All of a sudden out of the murky depths you feel something rough and cold nudge your leg. It is not necessary for you to stop and think that you must get out of the water as soon as possible. You don't have to decide to become afraid. The fear response is automatic because your mind has pictured a shark attacking you from under the water. The fear response caused by the mental image triggers bodily mechanisms that prepare your muscles to swim faster than you ever have before. Adrenalin, a powerful muscle stimulant, pours into your bloodstream. Your heartbeat speeds up. All bodily functions not needed for swimming shut down. For example, digestion is not important so your stomach stops working. All available blood is sent to the muscles. You begin breathing much faster, gulping in oxygen that is rushed to the muscles.

It is not important whether or not the thing that nudged you is a shark. You act, and feel, not according to what things really *are,* but according to the image your mind pictures— what things *seem to be*.

It would make absolutely no difference if the thing that nudged you was just a piece of seaweed or a harmless fish. As long as you thought and imagined the thing to be a great white shark, your emotional and nervous reactions would be exactly the same—you act automatically to what you *believe* to be true about yourself and your environment.

If our mental images of ourselves are distorted or unrealistic, then our reaction to our environment may also be inappropriate and unrealistic. Realizing that our actions, feelings, and behavior are the result of our own images and beliefs gives us the insight we need to improve personality traits. Think about it—it opens the psychological door to gaining skill, success, and happiness.

Forming mental pictures is an excellent way to create new personality traits and attitudes. This is possible because your nervous system cannot tell the difference between an actual experience and one that you vividly imagine. Let me say that again: *Your nervous system cannot tell the difference between an actual experience and one that you vividly imagine.* If we picture ourselves performing in a certain manner, it is almost the same as an actual performance. The following studies illustrate this point.

In a controlled experiment, R. A. Vandell proved that mental practice in throwing darts improves aim as much as actually throwing darts.

In another study, *Research Quarterly* reported that mental practice in making basketball free throws clearly demonstrated a positive effect on improving skill. The study involved three groups of students who were scored on their ability to shoot free throws, and then were scored again 20 days later. In the study, one group of college students practiced shooting free throws every day for the entire 20 days. Another group of students was not allowed to practice shooting at all. The third group of students spent 20 minutes a day *imagining* that they were shooting free throws.

The results were very interesting. The first group, which actually practiced 20 minutes every day, improved their scoring by 24 percent. The second group, which had no practice, showed no improvement. The third group, which practiced only in their imagination, improved their scoring by 23 percent. Notice that there was only 1 percentage point difference between those who actually practiced and those who practiced mentally.

Successful men and women have never been strangers to using mental pictures to rehearse or practice a skill. For example, Alexander the Great pictured his battles vividly in his mind before he actually went onto the battlefield. Napolean practiced soldiering in his imagination for years before he actually began any of his campaigns. He even went so far as to make notes that filled 400 pages. In these notes he imagined himself as commander and drew detailed maps of the island of Corsica, showing where he would place his defenses and making all his calculations with minute precision. Conrad Hilton imagined himself operating a hotel long before he ever bought one. Henry J. Kaiser realized his business accomplishments in his imagination before they actually occurred.

The technique worked for these well-known, successful people, and it will work for you. In fact, it has worked so well in the past that people who used mental picturing and then made those pictures come to pass were at one time thought to be witches or warlocks—this skill was considered black magic. You and I know that it is not magic; it is a part of the normal functioning of our minds.

Next time you attempt to do something important, try this idea. Rather than making a conscious effort to do the thing by iron-jawed willpower, simply relax. Stop trying to do it by superhuman effort. Instead, picture the goal you want to reach and let mental imagery work for you. When you form a mental picture of the desired result, it literally forces you to use positive thinking. Keep in mind that this does not relieve you from effort and work. It does, however, give you a goal, and your efforts will automatically carry you toward your goal. One of the major reasons we fail when we attempt to accomplish a task—such as losing weight, developing good study habits, or reaching financial goals—is that we concentrate on the day-to-day boring tasks. We concentrate on not eating dessert, or on sitting for tedious hours grinding out an English composition, or on depriving ourselves of pleasant luxuries so we can balance our budget.

When we use that "sweat-and-clenched-jaw" tactic to accomplish goals, more often than not we run out of sweat and our clenched jaw tires. The effort can't be sustained— there's not enough reward and satisfaction in the process, and we're thinking more of the task than of the goal. When you paint a vivid mental picture of your beautiful slim body, or your name being on the Dean's list, or being on a romantic Caribbean cruise when you have reached your financial goals, your resolve will remain strong because your momentum is carrying you toward a recognized goal that is meaningful to you—more meaningful than the drudgery of getting there.

This same creative mechanism within you can help you achieve your best possible self. You can form a picture in your imagination of the self you want to be and see yourself in that new role. This is a necessary condition for self-improvement. Before a person can change, one must somehow see oneself in that new role and be convinced that the ideal can become the reality.

Studies have proven it time and time again: your mental picture of yourself is the strongest force within you. Try it. What would you like to be? A calmer, less nervous person? A more studious person? A friendlier person? Close your eyes, relax, and create a mental motion picture of yourself as you would like to be. Do this every day. You might be surprised at the effect.

Guest Lecture 3
The Great Earthquake Mystery

Everyone loves a mystery. It might be a fictional one, such as "Who stabbed the millionaire while he was sipping brandy in his study when all the doors and windows were locked from the inside?" It might be a historical one, such as "Did Amelia Earhart's plane really crash, or is she possibly still alive?"

There are also mysteries of science, mysteries that are far broader in scope and much more important to mankind. In science, just as in police stories, there are detectives who gather clues—clues that are much harder to trace than a fingerprint left at the scene of the crime.

One of the great scientific mysteries of today is earthquakes. In ancient times, many people believed earthquakes were caused by angry gods to punish mankind. And who could predict or understand the mind of a whimsical god?

Other ancient people could not accept the idea that a god caused earthquakes. They suggested instead that huge giants were imprisoned underground. They believed that when these giants struggled to get out of their underground prisons, it caused earthquakes and volcanic eruptions. Since it was impossible to know when one of these giants was going to struggle, it was impossible to predict when an earthquake would occur.

Some ancient people suggested that the wind got lost and was trapped in caves. When the wind tried to blow itself out of those deep underground caves, it caused earthquakes. Since no one could know when or where the wind was going to be trapped, no one could predict when the next earthquake would occur.

Until relatively recent times, earthquakes were not of great concern. Big ones did not occur very often, and the earth was relatively unpopulated until just the last few hundred years. However, as the earth slowly became more populated, more buildings were built that could be destroyed by earthquakes. With the increased population came increased concern and dread of earthquakes.

On November 1, 1775, a great earthquake, possibly the most violent earthquake of modern times, struck the city of Lisbon, Portugal. That earthquake demolished every building in the lower part of the city. The quake, together with the giant tidal wave that it caused, killed 60,000 people. This earthquake was felt over an area of 1,500,000 square miles.

At the time of the Lisbon earthquake, scientific knowledge was growing rapidly. Scientists looked upon earthquakes with new understanding. In 1760, the English geologist John Mitchell suggested that earthquakes were caused by shifting masses of rock miles below the earth's surface. At last, scientists were on the right track to understanding the cause of earthquakes.

In 1855, the Italian physicist Luigi Palmieri devised the first seismograph. This instrument was able to measure the slightest tremors in the earth's crust. For the first time it became possible to record an earthquake and to calculate the spot at which it occurred. With this new instrument, scientists could also determine what areas were affected by an earthquake.

After the seismograph was invented, earthquake studies led to other important discoveries concerning our planet's inner structure. Through the study of earthquake waves, for example, we know that the earth has a liquid center made of iron and nickel.

We now know the places where earthquakes are most likely to occur. In the last few years we have come to understand that the earth's crust is made up of large tectonic plates. We know that earthquakes are most likely to occur where these plates join together.

One of the places where these plates meet is the San Andreas Fault that runs along the coast of California. There have been several disastrous earthquakes along this fault. The biggest earthquake to occur along this fault in modern times was the San Francisco earthquake of 1906.

When will the next great earthquake come? If it cannot be stopped, will we have enough warning to get everyone to safety before it happens?

The knowledge about earthquakes gathered in recent years has been tremendous, but it still isn't enough to let us know when one of the earth's plates will scrape against another and set the earth trembling. Most of the time the plates are wedged tightly against each other and held motionless. However, the strain slowly increases from year to year. Eventually, some slight nudge will set off a tremor that may cause another big earthquake. What will cause that nudge? Where will it come from? And when?

Doctors John Gribbon and Stephen Plaggeman are searching for clues on when that nudge will occur. Their hunt for clues has caused them to search and study not just the earth but also the sun and the entire solar system.

They have studied these clues very carefully, and they are still following them on a fascinating chase. They note such things as tiny changes—maybe a thousandth of a second—in the length of the day. They want to know what might cause that slight change. They consider explosions on the surface of the sun. They study explosions in more distant space that result in cosmic rays. They search for clues in the solid body of the earth and in the tides of the sun. Clues have led them to believe that there is a strange influence of the position of the planets on the earth. Perhaps someday soon, scientists will be able to predict when and where the next great earthquake will occur.

Meet difficulties with courage and overcome handicaps with character. It is not the difficulties but the power gained by rising above them that builds greatness and a place for leadership.

—Anonymous

Part 4

How to Study Your Textbook

Tomorrow's illiterate will not be the person who cannot read. Tomorrow's illiterate will be the person who has not learned how to learn.

— Alvin Toffler

A Winner Has to Be Only a Little Better

In life's endeavors, the difference between success and failure is often only a matter of inches. For example, in 1973 the great horse Secretariat won the Triple Crown of Thoroughbred racing. He became the undisputed champion, the king of horse racing. After winning the Triple Crown, Secretariat was retired to stud and syndicated for more than ten million dollars. There were several other excellent horses that ran against Secretariat, but when they were retired to stud, none was syndicated for more than one million dollars.

Secretariat was worth ten times more than any other horse. The reason he was worth ten times more is obvious: A ten-million-dollar horse can run ten times faster than a one-million-dollar horse. Right? Wrong! In fact, he cannot run twice as fast, or 25 percent faster, or even 5 percent faster than the other horses.

How much faster can a ten-million-dollar horse run than a one-million-dollar horse? The difference between victory and defeat in horse racing is usually only a very small margin. For example, when Secretariat won the Kentucky Derby, he was just *one second* ahead of Sham, the second place winner.

This general principle is also true for academic success or failure. On many tests, the difference between a D grade and a C grade can be one point. If you score 69 percent, you get a D; 70 percent earns you a C. The same is true of the difference between a C and a B grade, and a B and an A grade. Very often, just a tiny bit more effort can make you the ten-million-dollar champion.

As you approach the task of studying your textbook, keep in mind that a little extra effort can result in top grades, recognition, and a successful future. Approach the task of studying your textbook as a professional—just as a doctor, an accountant, or a professional athlete would approach their jobs. These respected professionals would never risk their reputations by attempting to perform their jobs without proper preparation and training. Neither should you. While you're a student, *studying* is your job, your profession. The only way you will rise to the top in your profession is to become highly skilled in that job.

Some students say, "Study? I'll just read through the textbook. That's all I need to do." That casual attitude may result in last-minute panic and complete loss of confidence before a test. As a result, those students stay up all night frantically reading and rereading the material in their textbooks. Don't fall into the trap of the casual, nonprofessional student. Learn to become a skilled professional at studying.

Some people think that the proper way to study a textbook takes too much time. Don't believe it! Nothing takes more time and causes more discouragement than reading and rereading six chapters to get ready for a test.

Learning to study a textbook properly will save you time and eliminate discouragement and frustration. When you progress through the material in your textbook using the proper study method, you will be learning the information as you go. You will also be getting ready for quizzes, tests, midterms, and finals. This organized and efficient way of studying will save you many hours of frantic and disorganized cramming for the big tests.

Questions for Discussion

1. "The difference between academic success and failure is often only a small margin." Explain the meaning of this statement.

2. A casual attitude toward reading your textbook may result in panic and loss of confidence. Why?

3. How can properly studying a textbook save you time?

Getting Ready to Study

When you think about reading a book, you might picture yourself relaxed in a comfortable chair or curled up on a cozy couch in front of a crackling fireplace. That's a beautiful way to enjoy a good book. But it is NOT the way to study a textbook. Reading for pleasure is one thing; studying for learning is quite another task.

Think about the sorts of books or magazines you choose for pleasure reading. Just as the name implies, pleasure reading is not intended to cause studious, intellectual reflection. It's entertaining, it's light, and it's usually easy reading. Maybe it's a fast-moving mystery or science fiction story that grabs your attention and keeps you riveted to the page. Or maybe it's a magazine that peeks into the lives of your favorite rock stars. In any case, it's something you read because you want to; it holds your attention because you're interested in it.

Unfortunately, the typical textbook is not written to hold the reader's attention with fast-paced plots or colorful human-interest stories. The reality is that most textbooks present facts, figures, and other meaningful information in a scholarly fashion. Their intent is to educate, not entertain you. Since the material is presented in a scholarly manner, the reader must approach it with a scholarly attitude. A scholarly attitude requires concentration, reflection, and attention to detail. It requires you to keep your attention on information that may not even be especially interesting to you.

When you're reading something because you *have* to, not because you *want* to, it's easy to let your mind wander. Research conducted by the Study Skills Institute discovered that in a typical 45-minute study period at home, many students actually studied for only 9 minutes. They spent the rest of the 45 minutes in daydreaming, thumbing through books, talking on the telephone, listening to music, and so forth. This means that 80 percent of the study period was wasted. If you are going to be a professional student, you need to handle your study sessions professionally.

Your primary job as a student is studying. As with any job, if you expect promotions, you must show up for work, do a good job while you're there, and maintain an appropriate work area.

It's especially important to have a work area set aside for the job of studying your textbook. You need a workbench or a desk—a place where pens, pencils, paper, and a dictionary are at your fingertips. You need a place where you can leave books open and papers ready for your next study session. You don't need a fancy desk; even a piece of plywood supported by two sawhorses can make a good place to study. And you don't need your own room; a corner of the living room or even the kitchen can serve the purpose. Abe Lincoln studied in a one room log cabin by the light of a fireplace. You can probably do better than that. In any case, having an official study area is important to your success as a professional student.

Having an official study area doesn't mean that's the *only* place you can study. In fact, you should study or review your material whenever and wherever you have the opportunity. Looking over your work during that extra 5 or 10 minutes you have at lunch time, for example, can be quite effective for brushup. Pioneer preachers were known to study their Bibles on horseback as they traveled between frontier towns. If you have a half-hour bus ride to school and back, why not use this time to read over your history assignment? Even so, you still need a regular place to study at home.

It is important to have a workplace that is used *only* for studying. Psychologists have demonstrated that if you nap or daydream too often while you're sitting at your desk, the desk will act as a cue or signal for you to nap or daydream as soon as you sit down. If you do nothing but *study* at your desk, however, your mind will automatically receive the signal to get down to serious studying whenever you sit there.

Having a proper place to study is very important, but following four additional rules will help you improve your performance as a skilled, professional student.

Rule 1. Keep the proper equipment at hand.

One handy piece of equipment to consider acquiring is a bookstand to hold your book open as you study. A bookstand can work for you in many ways. First, setting it up can give you a feeling of readiness to study. This alone is worth many times the price of the stand. Second, it eliminates the strain of continually holding the book open to the right page. Third, it frees your hands so you can take notes. Fourth, it allows you to sit back, think, and reflect on the meaning of what you are reading.

It is important to keep other study aids and supplies right at your desk. Some of the more important items are a good dictionary, a clock, a calendar, paper clips, tape, rubber bands, a supply of sharp pencils, erasers, and note cards. Having these items handy will help keep you sitting at your desk for the entire study period.

Perhaps this has happened to you: you are at your desk studying on the weekend when you begin to wonder how many more weeks there are before semester tests. You don't have a calendar at your desk, and the question continues to nag at you. Finally, you realize you are spending more time wondering "When is the end of the semester?" than you are studying. You get up and go into the kitchen to look at the calendar. While you're there, you decide to go outside to see what the weather is like. It's beautiful. Reluctantly, you come back inside, but decide to have a glass of milk just to keep from getting hungry. You slowly drink the milk and rinse the glass. Finally, half an hour later, you are back at your desk attempting to study, but by now you are out of the mood.

Do you recognize the negative effect of just one little interruption? If you keep your desk well supplied with all the study aids and supplies you may need, you will be less apt to find a tempting excuse to stop studying.

Rule 2. Use proper lighting in your study area.

The quality of light is of critical importance to good studying. Poor lighting causes tired eyes. Tired, strained eyes cause loss of concentration. Lighting engineers have found three things you should do to maintain good light in your study area:

• **Eliminate glare.** Studies show that reading by the light of an unshaded light bulb for three hours can cause a temporary loss of clear vision. Your study lamp should have a shade so the bulb does not shine directly in your eyes.

• **Eliminate light and dark areas of the room.** Shadows on your book will have a tiring effect on your eyes. Direct your study lamp to avoid shadows.

- **Eliminate flicker.** A flickering light will cause loss of concentration. In research conducted by the Study Skills Institute, it was discovered that students took 43 percent longer to learn material from a textbook if their lights were flickering. That means that a 45-minute study period would have to be stretched to more than an hour to make up for the lost concentration. Make sure your lights are functioning properly.

Rule 3.   Keep noise to a minimum.

Nothing is a greater waste of time than going over the same paragraph again and again because there is too much distraction—noise that prevents you from absorbing what you're reading. Noise is one of the most serious obstacles to effective study.

Some students claim that they can study better with background music. Don't fall into that trap. Studies conducted by Dr. R. Henderson found that students who preferred to study with music in the background actually understood less of the material they read than students who studied without background music.

Rule 4.   Do not set unrealistic goals.

Sometimes students postpone their studying because they promise themselves they will study for six hours the night before a test. Don't make that mistake. Most students find it difficult to study effectively for as long as three or four hours, much less six. If you leave all your studying for one long marathon session the night before a test, you are likely to be very disappointed with your test results.

Make yourself a reminder list that includes a schedule of the dates when reading assignments, papers, and other tasks are to be completed, and a plan for how you will complete them. For example, if on Monday you are given a 28-page reading assignment that must be completed by Friday, your reminder list might show that you need to read 7 pages a day in order to complete the schedule on time.   This sort of plan is also very useful when you have a long paper due in six weeks; it can help you get started before the last minute.

Setting up a place of study, obtaining the proper supplies and equipment, arranging satisfactory lighting, minimizing distracting noise, setting realistic goals, and organizing your schedule— all these preparations pave the way for serious and effective study. Then you can actually begin to study your textbook.

You've probably been studying for years, right? With all the practice you get, you would think you'd become better and better at it. Most students, however, find that the task does not become easier as time goes on. Instead, they feel like the oldtimer who said, "The hurrier I go, the behinder I get."

If you are having increasing difficulty with studying, in spite of all your practice, perhaps you are "using the wrong grip." Remember the first time you picked up a tennis racket? More than likely you held it with an incorrect grip. That bad grip weakened your stroke. You probably found that even with lots of practice, you did not improve your game. The same thing is true of your study method. A poor study method causes strain, and you usually don't improve even though you spend more time studying.

In the following pages, we will work on improving your grip (your study method) so you will get the results you want from study time. Keep in mind, however, that even with a good grip, you cannot improve your tennis game, or your study skills, without dedication and commitment.

Questions for Discussion

1.   Explain the difference between reading for pleasure and reading a textbook.

2.   Why do some students effectively study only 9 minutes out of a 45-minute study period?

3.   Why is it important to have a workplace that is used only for studying?

4.   What are some important study aids and supplies you should have at your desk?

5.   What are the three things you should do to maintain good lighting in your study area?

6.   Why is noise a serious obstacle to effective study?

7.   To make sure you do not set unrealistic study goals, you should make yourself a reminder list. What should that list include?

Courage is the first of human qualities because it is the quality which guarantees all the others.
— Winston Churchill

It's Not Necessary to Read a Textbook Again and Again

Have you ever read a paragraph in your textbook, then realized that you remember absolutely nothing about what you read? Most students emphatically nod their heads "Yes!" in response to that question. You probably have also had that experience.

Studies have shown that when students read a textbook without a structured method of study, most of them remember less than 2 percent of the material after two weeks. The reason you often cannot remember what you've read is that your brain does not "see" the words on the page.

Your brain can absorb text at the rate of about 1800 to 2000 words per minute. The typical student reads at 250 to 400 words per minute. The unfortunate result is that while your eyes are crawling across the page so slowly, your mind gets bored. It takes a mini-vacation and goes someplace else—to the mountains, the beach, or the lake. It starts wondering, "How many more pages do I have to read?" When that happens, your body and eyes are reading at your desk, but you're actually "mindless." Your eyes are tracking across the page, but your mind is not registering or seeing the words. That's why you have to read the text several times, concentrating hard to get your mind to focus on and understand what you're reading.

How do you overcome this problem? The best way is to entice your brain into giving your eyes its undivided attention for short, but effective, periods of time. This can be accomplished fairly easily. Let's eavesdrop on an imaginary conversation taking place between the brain and eyes as you are trying to complete a textbook reading assignment.

Your eyes are saying, "Brain, we've got to talk. We're getting fed up with your irresponsibility! You constantly leave us while we are reading. We can never depend on you. Look, we can't get through this reading assignment without your help. We'll be sitting here all night unless you start focusing your attention on this chapter."

The brain arrogantly replies, "It's not my fault that you can't keep up with me. I'm a highly complex organ—I'm imaginative, I'm dynamic! I can't waste my time slow-poking around with you. If you want my help, you've got to keep me busy, and active, and interested!"

The eyes brighten. "If that's all you need, then we really don't have a problem. We'll make a deal with you. If you'll give us your undivided attention while we read just one paragraph, we'll agree to stop reading for a while and you can do something else with that paragraph. Is it a deal?"

The brain looks doubtful. "Well . . . I guess we can try it. But don't expect me to give you my full attention for more than one paragraph at a time. If you try to read an entire page without letting me do something interesting, I'll take off again."

The eyes bat gleefully. "It's a deal!"

It may sound silly, but it's really a very practical way of keeping your mind on task when you're studying. In the following pages, you'll read about some ways to keep your brain busy, and active, and interested while you're reading a textbook.

Questions for Discussion

1. When students read a textbook without a structured method of study, most of them remember less than 2 percent of the material after two weeks. Explain why this can happen.

2. How can your body and your eyes be "mindless" when you read?

3. How can you overcome the problem of not being able to focus your attention on the words of your textbook?

> A person's mind stretched to a new idea
> never goes back to its original dimension.
> — Oliver Wendell Holmes

The Professional Way to Study Your Textbook

Reading a textbook requires the use of your brain as well as your eyes. With the use of both these important parts of your head, you can begin to read the same way scholars read.

How do scholars read? Scholars know two important things about studying a textbook. First, they know they must question and analyze as they read. Scholars know that simply reading words does not necessarily mean they comprehend the material. When they question and analyze as they read, their comprehension is increased because they have enticed their brains to become actively involved.

Second, scholars know that they cannot possibly remember everything they have read. They know they must use a reading method that will allow them to find important information again later without having to search through the entire textbook.

The reading method that will help you read the same way successful scholars read is called the TI-3R method (say it "Tee-Eye-Three-R"). TI-3R is an abbreviated way of saying "Think, Index, Read, Record, Recite." Or, looking at it another way:

    T = Think
    I = Index
    3R = Read, Record, Recite

With this reading method, you will entice your brain to follow your eyes across the page of a textbook; you will increase your comprehension because you will question and analyze as you read; and you will be able to locate important information in your textbook without searching through page after page.

The TI-3R Method

Let's examine the steps of the TI-3R method so you can understand and begin to use it.

T = Think

Just as a gymnast would never consider doing a tumbling exercise without stretching and warming up first, neither should you try the mental exercise of reading from your textbook without first warming up. Your mental warm-up is simply taking 10 to 20 seconds to *think* about what you are going to read. You must think about what you are going to read in a special way, a *personal* way. For example, if you were to sit down to read a textbook chapter about the causes of World War II, you might warm up by thinking about someone you know who was in that war. Perhaps you would think about the kind of cars people drove in those days or the kind of clothes they wore. This warm-up activity will help you take your mind off whatever you were involved in before you began to read. Unless you warm up first, it takes your mind at least ten minutes to forget your previous activity and to begin to focus on your reading.

In studies conducted by the Study Skills Institute, it was discovered that when students used the mental warm-up exercises, they remembered eleven times more of the textbook material than they otherwise would. This means that if you normally remember two pieces of information from reading a textbook assignment, you may well remember 22 pieces of information if you use mental warm-ups.

I = Index

Indexing is the simplest procedure in the TI-3R method, but in many ways it's the most important. To index your textbook, simply begin with the first paragraph on the first page of your reading assignment and number each paragraph. The index

1   Who is better at predicting earthquakes: animals or scientists with instruments? Evidence collected so far suggests that an ordinary animal—a dog, a horse, a pig—may give as reliable a warning of an impending earthquake as the scientists.

2   In 1979, 200 instruments failed to predict a California earthquake that shook buildings in San Francisco, 78 miles away. But in 1974, several months before a massive earthquake in China, pigs climbed the walls, hens would not roost, trained dogs ignored commands, and barnyard geese refused to fly. The Chinese heeded these and other signs and evacuated people before the quake struck, thereby saving several hundred thousand lives.

3   In the past few years, instruments have successfully predicted earthquakes in Mexico and Asia, but scientists are taking no chances. Many nations now have animal warning centers to try to learn what it is that the animals sense so that instruments can be built to detect the same signals.

44

Figure 6. Indexing a textbook page.

number should be written very lightly *in pencil* in the outside margin. You will need to erase these numbers at the end of the term or school year if the textbook belongs to your school.

The first complete paragraph on each page begins with the number 1. That is, each page is numbered separately. Figure 6 illustrates the proper way to index a page of your textbook.

There are three reasons why indexing your textbook is important:

1. Indexing provides a fast and easy way to locate information in your textbook, as will be described in the following pages.

2. Indexing paves the way to a very efficient way of studying for a test.

3.   Indexing breaks your reading into bite-sized chunks so you are not intimidated by the thought of having to deal with an entire chapter. When you index, you are faced with understanding only one paragraph at a time.

R = Read

When reading a textbook, the only thing different from other reading you may do is that you read and understand a textbook one paragraph at a time. You should read each paragraph with this thought in mind: "What did the author say in this paragraph?" Then, in your own words, attempt to answer that question. Do not go on to the next paragraph until you can.

R = Record

Once you know what was said in the paragraph, it's time to make up a question from the paragraph and record your question on a three- by five-inch note card or piece of paper. It is very important to formulate a question that can be answered by the material in the paragraph.

"Why a question?" you might ask. "Wouldn't outlining or writing the topic sentence work just as well?"

Research conducted by the Study Skills Institute revealed that the act of writing a question is much more effective as a study tool than writing a topic sentence or outlining. Formulating a question requires you to think about the information in the paragraph. If you don't know what you read, it is nearly impossible to ask a good question. A good question requires knowledge of the subject. On the other hand, you *don't* need to know the material to outline or write the topic sentence, because you can simply copy from the book. Copying topic sentences, or even outlining, does not help you understand the material you are reading.

A good way to pose a question about a paragraph is to pretend you are a teacher. Ask yourself, "What question would I ask my students if I wanted to make sure they understood the paragraph?" For example, a good question for paragraph 1 in the illustration on page 83 might be: "What does the evidence suggest about the ability of animals to predict earthquakes?" It is very important that you *do not* ask a question that can be answered yes or no. A yes-or-no question will not help you remember the material in the paragraph.

Once you have formulated a question, record it in the following manner:

1.   Write the question on a three- by five-inch index card.

2.   Assign an index number to the card. This number is very important. Later when you review, you will want to know where each question came from in your textbook, in case you need to check the answer. The index number will tell you exactly where to look. The number you assign to the card has two parts: the index number you gave to the paragraph, and the textbook page number on which the paragraph appears.   In this example, the question came from paragraph 1 on page 44 of the textbook. Therefore, you would assign this card the number 1-44. Your completed index card should look like the first one in figure 7.

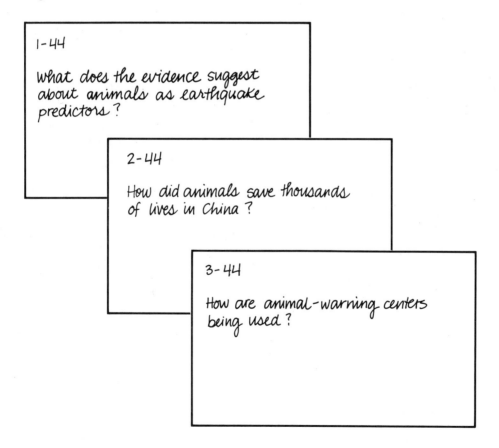

Figure 7.   Recording questions as you read a textbook.

3. Go back and make sure you can find the answer to your question in the paragraph. In this example, the answer contained in the paragraph is, "Evidence collected so far suggests that an ordinary animal—a dog, a horse, a pig—may give as reliable a warning of an impending earthquake as scientists."

Using the TI-3R method for all the text about earthquakes shown in figure 6, you might make the three index cards shown in figure 7. Notice how the index numbers are assigned. Read the three paragraphs again (page 83) to find the answers to the index-card questions.

R = Recite

This step of the TI-3R method is crucial to its success. When you have finished your reading assignment, close your textbook and ask yourself the index-card questions. Without looking at your textbook, recite the answers out loud. Always recite the answers *out loud* to reinforce your understanding and to prove to yourself that you know the material. It is not necessary that you know 100 percent of the answers. Remember, you are only reviewing, not studying for a test at this point.

> **NOTE: It is very important that you *do not* write answers on the back of your paragraph index cards.** Writing answers on the back of the cards will greatly reduce the effectiveness of this study method. Why? Because if the answers are too easy for you to refer to, you will read them and think you know the material when, in fact, you do not.

Always end your reading assignment by reciting from the index cards. This recitation is an effective way to summarize and imprint the information on your mind.

TI-3R: Another Example

Let's run through the TI-3R method again, with a sample assignment, to be sure you understand the five steps.

T = Think

Suppose you are going to read a textbook assignment for your Personal Health class. The chapter is called "Rules for Successful

Conversation." Your mental warm-up for this assignment might include such thoughts as these:

- "I want to be popular, so I should learn how to be a good conversationalist."

- "Why is it important for me to learn the rules of successful conversation?"

- "What person has impressed me as a good conversationalist?"

If you use any, or all, of these mental warm-ups before you begin to read this assignment, your mind will be ready to go to work. In all three warm-ups you are forcing yourself to think about the assignment in a personal way. That is, the warm-ups all relate to your personal interests. These exercises will take your mind off your previous activity and focus it on your textbook assignment.

I = Index

When you index a reading assignment, you simply number each paragraph very lightly in pencil. The first page of this sample reading assignment appears on the following page in figure 8. Note that the index numbers have already been written beside the paragraphs.

R = Read

Now read the first paragraph of this sample assignment with one question in mind: "What is the author saying to me?" Do not move ahead to the next paragraph until you can answer that question.

R = Record

Once you have read the paragraph and understand what the author is saying, it's time to formulate a specific question from the paragraph and record it, along with an index number, on a three- by five-inch card. A possible question from paragraph 1 might be, "What is the first rule of successful conversation and why is it important?"

Rules for Successful Conversation

The First Rule of Successful Conversation

1   The first rule of successful conversation is, "Listen to other people who are talking." By listening carefully to others, you may learn what things interest them. When you know what interests people, you can relate to those areas of interest. This will increase your popularity because people like someone who responds to their interests.

2   Of course, the more you listen, the more you can learn about other people. Listening requires you to be silent; you can't talk and listen at the same time. An old Latin proverb gives a clue to the value of silence: "Keep quiet and people will think you are a philosopher." Silence should not be overdone, however, because real listening requires proof. After the person who is speaking pauses, ask a question or give your feelings and opinion about what was said. Obviously you cannot make comments or ask questions unless you listen. Your comments and questions are the proof that you were listening. This technique will assure your popularity.

The Second Rule of Successful Conversation

3   The second rule of successful conversation is, "Ask questions." When you ask questions that require the other person to give an opinion or make an evaluation, you show that you respect the other person's opinion. People always like to be asked for their opinions.

4   Obviously, your questions must be sincere. If you attempt to fool people by pretending to have respect for what they say when none exists, they will see through you and you will lose rather than gain popularity.

5   The best way to demonstrate sincerity in your questioning is to ask questions that will increase your knowledge. An old English proverb points out the fallacy of insincere questions: "A fool can ask more questions in an hour than a wise man can ask in a year."

The Third Rule of Successful Conversation

6   The third rule of successful conversation is, "Talk about the other person's plans and goals." You can become a more successful conversationalist by simply asking people to tell you their plans for the future or their important goals. Most people are usually happy to talk about their future and the exciting things they have planned.

7   If you have a problem trying to think of something to say, simply concentrate on the other person. Concentrate on getting the other person talking about his or her plans and goals. Once the conversation starts, your own thoughts will be stimulated by what you hear.

312

Figure 8.   Sample reading assignment.

Look carefully at this question. Is it a yes-or-no question? Can the answer to the question be found in paragraph 1? If it is not a yes-or-no question, and if the answer can be found in the paragraph, it is probably a good question.

Your completed index card for this paragraph might look like the example in figure 9.

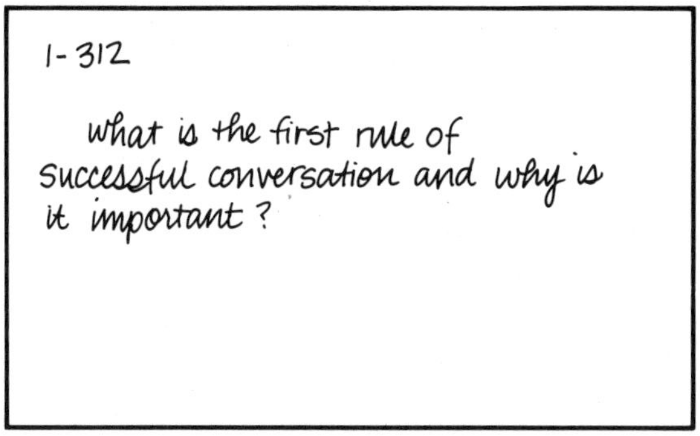

Figure 9. A textbook index card for the first paragraph.

Now you can proceed to paragraph 2. You don't need to do the T = Think step or the I = Index step with paragraph 2 or with any other paragraphs in the reading assignment because these two steps are done only when you begin an assignment.

Now read paragraph 2 in figure 8, trying to understand what the author is saying to you. Have you read it? This paragraph actually makes two important points. It refers to an old Latin proverb, and it suggests how you can prove you are listening. For this paragraph you will probably want to formulate two questions and write them on two separate index cards. Some possible questions from paragraph 2 might be, "What does an old Latin proverb say about silence?" and "How can I prove that I am listening?" (See figure 10 on the following page to see how you might assign index numbers to the cards for these two questions.)

Are these yes-or-no questions? Can the answers to these questions be found in the paragraph? If they are not yes-or-no questions, and if the answers can be found in the paragraph, they are probably good questions.

You would continue through the entire assignment one paragraph at a time, doing the R = Read and R = Record steps. Remember, you must understand what the author is saying in each paragraph before you proceed to the next.

Your completed index cards for the sample assignment might look like the examples shown in figure 10. Carefully analyze the questions. Are any of them yes-or-no questions? Can the answers to all the questions be found in the paragraphs? Are these all good questions? If not, which ones would you reword, and how?

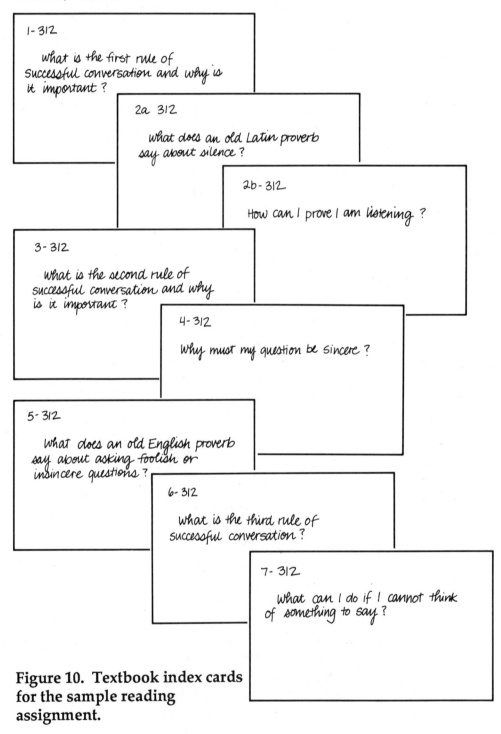

1- 312

what is the first rule of successful conversation and why is it important ?

2a 312

what does an old Latin proverb say about silence ?

2b- 312

How can I prove I am listening ?

3- 312

what is the second rule of successful conversation and why is it important ?

4- 312

Why must my question be sincere ?

5- 312

what does an old English proverb say about asking foolish or insincere questions ?

6- 312

what is the third rule of successful conversation ?

7- 312

What can I do if I cannot think of something to say ?

Figure 10. Textbook index cards for the sample reading assignment.

R = Recite

This is the fifth and final step of the TI-3R method for reading a textbook. To recite, set the reading assignment aside, go back to your index cards, and recite the answers to your questions out loud. It is important to do this out loud. If you recite the answers silently to yourself, it's easy to *think* you know the material when, in fact, you do not. It is important to hear yourself say the answers. Reciting is a very important step because it helps you quickly and effectively summarize the important points of the assignment. Reciting helps lock the material in your mind. Try it. Can you recite the answers to the questions in figure 10?

Textbook Study Practice Exercises

Following are two more sample reading assignments to give you practice in the TI-3R method for studying a textbook. Before you begin, let's quickly review the five steps of TI-3R.

Think   Mental warm-up. Think about the reading material in a personal way.

Index   Number the paragraphs very lightly in pencil.

Read   Read each paragraph with one question in mind: "What is the author saying?"

Record   Formulate a question about each paragraph and assign it an index number. Record your question and number on a three- by five-inch card. Remember, never ask yes-or-no questions, and always make sure you can find the answer to your question in the corresponding paragraph.

Recite   Close your book and recite the answers to your questions on index cards. Remember, never write answers on the backs of your cards.

Go through all five steps of the TI-3R method for the following two sample reading assignments: a science assignment about hurricanes, and a history assignment about Albert

Einstein. Write your paragraph questions on note cards and be sure to assign index numbers. Just for these exercises, do the first "Think" step in writing, listing some things you might think about as a mental warm-up before you begin reading. Remember to think about the subject in a personal way.

Sample Assignment 1

Hurricanes

In the summer months, after the southern seas begin to warm, hurricane season begins. The Gulf of Mexico, the Caribbean Sea, and the Atlantic Ocean southeast of Florida are prime locations for hurricanes.

A hurricane is a large, traveling, tropical storm accompanied by high winds and torrential rains. The huge storms can be very destructive, with winds ranging from 75 to 200 miles per hour.

Hurricanes are usually circular in shape. They average from 300 to 500 miles in diameter. In the center of the storm the air is calm and the sky is clear. This center area is known as the "eye" of the hurricane.

As the storm begins over the tropical southern seas, it appears in satellite photographs as a dark swirling donut of clouds. Weather experts study the satellite pictures to determine the direction and intensity of the storm.

Hurricanes are identified and named in alphabetical order. The first hurricane of the season is given a name beginning with the letter A, such as Albert. The second hurricane is given a name beginning with the letter B, such as Bonnie. The third might be named Carl, and so on until the hurricane season is over.

When a hurricane blows ashore in populated coastal areas, damage is often extensive. Trees may be blown through roofs and power lines. Strong winds often demolish buildings, and heavy seas have been known to send boats crashing into the middle of towns. At times, the area may be under several feet of water.

Luckily, weather experts can predict with a high degree of accuracy when a hurricane will strike land. Weather satellites take pictures of storm danger areas. Airplanes fly over suspicious-looking clouds. Temperature, pressure, humidity, and winds are closely watched. Experts using these methods are able to predict the build-up and movement of hurricanes. They issue storm warnings so people will have a chance to prepare for the storm and leave if necessary. No one can stop a hurricane, but early warnings save many lives.

156

Sample Assignment 2

78

Albert Einstein and the Atom Bomb

The creation of the atom bomb was one of the most important scientific events in modern history. It completely changed our concept of warfare and has become the predominant force in international strategy. Who was responsible for this awesome weapon that has so influenced the world? Strangely enough, the man who was basically responsible for the atom bomb was a pacifist for much of his life. However, it was his letter to President Franklin D. Roosevelt that started our development of the atomic bomb.

One night in 1939 Albert Einstein wrote what was to be one of the most important letters in American history. In his letter to President Roosevelt, Einstein wrote, "Recent work leads me to expect that the element uranium may be turned into a new and important source of energy in the immediate future. . . . This new phenomenon would also lead to the construction of bombs." Based on the information in this letter, President Roosevelt authorized the Manhattan Project to develop the atomic bomb, and the United States entered history's most deadly race for a military weapon.

Throughout most of his life Albert Einstein was pursued by things he did not want—publicity, fame, and offers of money and power. He was constantly surrounded by misunderstanding and controversy. Hundreds of scientists have spent countless hours trying to disprove his theories. He was a staunch believer in individual freedom and in democratic institutions, yet he was accused of being a communist. He had an unshakable faith in God, but he was called an atheist.

As a man of science, he was astonished when he was offered thousands of dollars to endorse products ranging from cough medicines to refrigerators. He was honored by colleges and universities throughout the world. A beautiful monument has been erected to him in Germany.

He is the only American citizen to be offered the presidency of another nation. All this came to a man who asked only for the solitude to think and work. "I'm happy because I want nothing from anyone," he once said. He added, "But I do get pleasure from the appreciation of my fellow workers."

A Move to the United States

In 1933, the Nazi government was coming to power in Germany. Einstein, who was 54 years old, left his native Germany to come to the United States. He settled in Princeton, New Jersey, where he joined the staff of the Institute for Advanced Study. He found peace in Princeton and he was happy in his work. His fellow workers didn't object that he wore his hair long, knowing that it was simply because he wouldn't take the time to go to the barber. They didn't mind that he dressed for comfort in unpressed trousers and a loose pullover sweater, sometimes with an old necktie in place of a belt. Fellow scientists said of him, "Even when discussing theoretical physics he radiates humor, warmth, and kindness."

Einstein worked in a big, comfortable office with a peaceful view of woods and nature. There he was absorbed for many years in working out his Unified Field Theory. This theory connects the two great forces of our physical universe—gravitation and electromagnetism—and shows the relationship between all known physical phenomena.

When blocked by a problem, Einstein stayed with it. Sometimes he would twirl strands of his uncombed hair around a finger. Each of his theories was the result of months and years of stubborn persistence, which he called "idealized experiments." Pencil and paper were his scientific equipment; his mind was his laboratory. He sometimes came to wrong conclusions, but he worked hard to correct them and he never gave up.

He believed the correct answer was sure to be found. "God is subtle, but never mischievous," he often said. Einstein believed in the simplicity and logical orderliness of nature. When he weighed his own conclusions, he asked himself, "Could this be the way God created the universe?"

A Man with Humility

In spite of his greatness and brilliant intellect, Einstein was humble and shy. When he addressed a conference in Washington, every person in the room stood and applauded. Taken aback, he whispered to a friend, "I think they ought to wait to hear what I say." At a dinner in his honor, speaker after speaker gave glowing accounts of his genius. Einstein squirmed uncomfortably. Finally he turned to the person sitting next to him and said, "You know, I never wear socks." It was his way of bringing himself down to earth.

When he was offered the chance to become President of Israel, Einstein said that he felt unqualified for a job that involved human relations. He said he thought it would be better to continue his study of the physical world, of which he had "a little comprehension."

Einstein was born on March 14, 1879, at Ulm, Germany. He grew up in Munich. Einstein was so slow to learn to talk that his parents thought he was abnormal. Teachers considered him a misfit because he had few friends and avoided games. For fun, he composed little religious songs on the piano. He often hummed them as he walked alone through the woods around Munich.

By the age of 12, Einstein was pursuing independent studies in science and mathematics. Although he was brilliant in mathematics and physics, he had no aptitude for languages. He failed his first attempt to pass the polytechnic college entrance exam. He tried again a year later and finally passed.

During the two years after he graduated from college, Einstein was fired from three teaching jobs. He was often without money. He married Mileva Marec, who was also a science student. They eventually had two sons. Finally, he was hired as an examiner in the patent office of Bern, Switzerland. It was a simple job, and it allowed him to concentrate on his own studies. He was trying to link time, space, matter, and energy. Sometimes he became discouraged; on the very day before he found the solution he even told a friend, "I'm going to give it up."

The Famous Equation

At the age of 26, although unknown in the scientific world, he submitted his "Theory of Relativity" to a physics journal. He expressed his theory in what is now the most famous equation of science: $E=mc^2$. The equation demonstrated that if all the energy in one-half pound of any matter were released, the resulting power would equal the explosive force of seven million tons of dynamite. Although it revolutionized our understanding of the universe, few physicists realized its staggering importance. For years $E=mc^2$ was a lively topic for debate. When the first atomic bomb exploded on Hiroshima, it became a deadly reality.

In the 1930s, many scientists knew that Nazi Germany was working around the clock to develop atomic energy. American scientists appealed to military leaders to tackle a similar project. They were not successful in their plea. The scientists asked Einstein to use his influence. As a result, in 1939 he wrote his fateful letter to President Roosevelt.

Albert Einstein died at Princeton on April 18, 1955, at the age of 76. He was still seeking answers to secrets of time and space. Even though he knew no one could ever know everything, he believed that "One of the most beautiful things man can experience is the search for answers in the universe."

Everyone sits in a prison of his own ideas; he must burst it open and try to test his ideas on reality.

—Albert Einstein

Suggestions for Marking Textbooks

Although most students who attend public schools are not allowed to write in their textbooks, those of you who plan to continue on to college could benefit from learning how to highlight, underline, and mark the textbooks you will be buying. The following suggestions will help you study as you read a textbook that you own.

1. Use a single line under words or phrases to signify important material. For example:

> Tremors of appreciable violence that occur within the earth are called earthquakes.

2. Circle key words. For example:

> There are many causes for tremors within the upper rocks of the lithosphere.

3. Use small circled numbers above initial words of an underlined group of words to indicate a series of facts or ideas. For example:

> The most common are faulting of rocks, volcanic explosions, falling in of the roofs of large underground caverns, and slumping of the fronts of steep submarine deltas.

4. Too much underlining can make the material hard to read. Therefore, when you come across three or more important lines in a row, use a vertical line in the outer margin rather than underlining them all. For example:

> Earthquakes are measured by a very sensitive instrument called a seismograph, which records the shocks waves on a revolving drum of paper. A styllus is suspended above the drum so that when an earthquake occurs, the styllus remains stable while the drum moves back and forth with the motion of the earth.

5. Place asterisks (*) in the margin next to ideas or facts of unusual importance.

6. Place a question mark in the margin next to lines you do not understand, as a reminder to ask the teacher for clarification.

7.   If you disagree with a statement, write the word *disagree* in the margin to remind you to discuss it with the teacher.

8.   Using sheets of paper that are smaller than the pages of the book, write longer thoughts you may have about the reading, or summaries of the material, and insert these sheets between the pages.

Questions for Discussion

1.   What does TI-3R stand for?

2.   What should you do to properly perform the "Think" step of the TI-3R method?

3.   Why is the "Think" step of the TI-3R method so important?

4.   How do you index a textbook page when you use the TI-3R method?

5.   Give three reasons why indexing your textbook is important.

6.   When you read a paragraph using the TI-3R method, you should read it with one thought in mind. What is that thought?

7.   What is the second "R" of the TI-3R method?

8.   Why is recording a question more effective than outlining or writing the topic sentence?

9.   What is a good way to pose a question from a paragraph?

10. What are the three steps of recording your question?

11. How do you do the "Recite" step of the TI-3R method?

12. Why is the "Recite" step important?

13. Why should you never put answers on the backs of your index cards?

Make the most of yourself, for that is all there is of you.
—Ralph Waldo Emerson

Part 5

How to Study for Tests

To prepare well is to succeed.
                —Benjamin Franklin

Studying for Test Success

When a test is coming up, many students believe they must go back and reread the entire textbook, decipher pages of lecture notes, and memorize endless lists of terms and definitions. Does that sound familiar? This study method can cause panic and even failure because it's difficult to accomplish all these things in the short time you probably have available for studying.

In this section you will learn how to condense and organize the material you need to study for a test. With this method, the studying you do will take you less time and will be more effective. You will learn how to use your memory keys from class notes and your index cards from reading assignments to efficiently cover everything you need to review and learn for a test.

Students usually begin to study for a test with determination and enthusiasm—qualities necessary if they are to earn high scores. Frequently, though, they become discouraged or lose interest before they finish their preparation. The result is a low test score. If those students were able to maintain a high level of interest and enthusiasm, the result would be much different: they would probably earn that desired high score.

When you set out to accomplish a task, you need to provide yourself with built-in motivators. The motivators will help you maintain your resolve and enthusiasm, and will keep you working toward your objective.

For example, suppose you are going to take a trip to visit your best friend who recently moved 300 miles away. You are going to be driven to your friend's house in the back of a closed van that has no windows, so it is impossible for you to see out. When you begin the trip, you enthusiastically anticipate seeing your good friend. But as the trip continues, you become slightly bored; it seems you've been travelling for an awfully long time. If you could only see out, you could judge how much farther you have to go. The trip continues, and soon you lose your sense of direction. You can't see the road signs. You wonder if you're even on the right road. Before long, you forget the prospect of a pleasant visit with your friend. You're bored, and your enthusiasm has turned to frustration. Boredom and frustration, combined with the nagging feeling that you're probably on the wrong road, make you want to stop the van and get out. The journey is so boring and confusing that you wish you'd never started.

You may experience the same feelings when you study for a test. After a few hours, you become bored because you are not sure how much more studying you need to do to get an A or B. That boredom, combined with the nagging feeling that you might not even be studying the right material, can cause you to lose your enthusiasm and make you want to give up.

A defeatist attitude like this can be prevented if you have a way of gauging your progress toward your goal and if you can be sure you are studying the right material. In this section you will be learning a method that can give you both: a way to gauge your progress and assurance that you are studying the right material.

Questions for Discussion

1. Why do some students become discouraged and lose interest before they finish studying for a test?

2. How does the story about riding in a van to visit a friend relate to studying for a test?

> **O Lord, thou givest everything at the price of an effort.**
> —**Leonardo da Vinci**

Don't Be a Counterfeiter

There was a fine artist who lived in the late 1800s. This man was such an accomplished artist that he could actually handpaint $20 bills. He painted $20 bills so realistically that he could use them to purchase supplies at the small general store near his home. He did this for several years before he was caught. Eventually, of course, he was arrested.

After he was arrested, police searched his home. In the attic, they found a $20 bill he had started to paint. They also found some portraits he had painted. These portraits were so beautiful that they later sold at auction for several thousand dollars.

The irony of this true story is that it took this fine artist almost the same length of time to paint a $20 bill as it took him to paint a portrait worth several thousand dollars.

This man was a thief in every sense of the word. But the real tragedy of the story is that he stole more from himself than from anyone else. He could have been a wealthy man if he had spent his time painting portraits instead of painting $20 bills.

Many students behave like this counterfeiter. They steal from themselves. Student "counterfeiting" can take several forms. See if you recognize any of them.

One form of counterfeiting occurs when you don't stick to business. You set aside an hour to study for a test. You look at the clock at the beginning of the study period and resolve to stick with it. But during that time period you call friends, take a peek at a television program your family is watching, daydream, and take several minutes to count how many pages you have left to study. At the end of the hour you close your books and end your study period—without anywhere near an hour's worth of study. When you fall into the trap of not sticking to business, you rob yourself of valuable time.

Another form of counterfeiting you may recognize is "avoiding the hard stuff." With this counterfeit method you spend almost all your time reviewing the material you already know. If you aren't careful, you may do this unintentionally. It's natural to take the path of least resistance. To avoid this error, make a list of everything you must study for the test and check off each item as you master it.

One other form of counterfeiting is called cheating. Cheating usually occurs when you lack confidence in yourself as a student. It's risky and very dangerous. Beware of cheating because it robs you in the most vicious way. It can rob you of your test score and even your privilege to attend school if you get caught. It also robs you of an opportunity to learn important information. But perhaps most important, it robs you of your self-respect and self-esteem.

Keep in mind that using counterfeit methods to study for a test takes as much time, or even more time, than good productive preparation. These counterfeit techniques may get you through a test, but the result is usually a low grade. The time you spend on the test is a painful waste of time instead of a valuable learning experience.

The method you are about to learn—using "Solitaire Lay-Down Cards"—removes the temptation to resort to counterfeit techniques and unproductive shortcuts. It also offers you a building-block approach to learning, in that the cards you prepare for one exam will serve as useful review for later exams. When you use this method to study for a test, you will have your material in such good order that midterms and final exams will be a breeze.

Questions for Discussion

1. Discuss some shortcuts you may be using to study for tests that could be termed "counterfeit methods."

2.   "Some students are like the counterfeiter. They steal from themselves when they use counterfeit methods to study for tests." Discuss the meaning of this statement.

> **The biggest mistake in the world is to think we are working for someone else.**
> **—Anonymous**

Solitaire Lay-Down Cards

Some of you may have already discovered on your own the following way to study for a test. You start out by preparing a set of "cheat notes" that cover everything you need to know for the test—with no intention, of course, of using them to actually cheat. You carefully review these notes to make sure you have included absolutely everything you will need for the test. Then you throw them away and take the test without them. It's an excellent way to review and learn material.

There's an even better method, though, that has more built-in motivators and that also helps you gauge your progress in studying for a test—two features that will help you maintain your enthusiasm and keep from getting discouraged. This method is the use of Solitaire Lay-Down Cards. You make these cards yourself using only your memory keys from your class notes and the index-card questions you prepared while reading your textbook.

In addition to being useful when you study for an individual test, Solitaire Lay-Down Cards have another important advantage: the deck of cards you prepare for one test becomes a ready-made tool you can use later to study for midterms and finals. By the time you need to start studying for midterms and final exams, much of your work will already be done. Sound good? Here's how to make those time-saving cards.

Six Steps for Making Solitaire Lay-Down Cards

To demonstrate how to make a deck of Solitaire Lay-Down Cards, let's assume you are preparing for a unit test in your physical science class. Assume that one of the lectures you will be tested on is the sample lecture called "The Great Earthquake Mystery," which was presented on pages 66-68 of this book.

Step 1.   Refer back to your class notes.

If you practiced taking "lecture notes" on that sample lecture about earthquakes, you may want to use them for reference. If not, it would be a good idea to glance through that lecture now before you proceed, then take a quick look at the set of sample notes for that lecture, shown in figure 11.

Step 2.   Number each page of your lecture notes.

Place a page number in the upper right-hand corner of each page of the lecture notes you need to study for the test.

Step 3.   Discard.

In almost all card games, players discard those cards they think they will not need. The same thing applies when you make Solitaire Lay-Down Cards.

The reason you can discard some cards, or information, from the deck is because you are now much smarter than you were when you first wrote your class notes. When you wrote your notes, that may have been the first time you ever heard the information. But after several class discussions, you are probably very familiar with some of the material and understand it thoroughly. If you completely understand portions of your notes, you won't need to study them further.

To discard, simply read through your memory key notes very carefully. When you come to material you know so well that you are *sure* you don't need to study it further, put a large check (✓) next to the memory key. The check indicates that the memory key is a discard and will not need to be studied.

Step 4.   Number in order each memory key of your lecture notes, skipping the discards.

Beginning with the first memory key at the top of the page, number all your memory keys except the ones you have dis-carded. When you have completed the first four steps your lecture notes will look like the example shown in figure 11.

Step 5.   Prepare the first half of your deck of Solitaire Lay-Down Cards.

Get out a three- by five-inch index card (or a piece of paper

Step 1: Refer back to your lecture notes.

Step 2: Number each page of your lecture notes.

Step 3: Discard. Make a check mark next to memory keys you will not need to study.

Step 4: Number each memory key, skipping the discards.

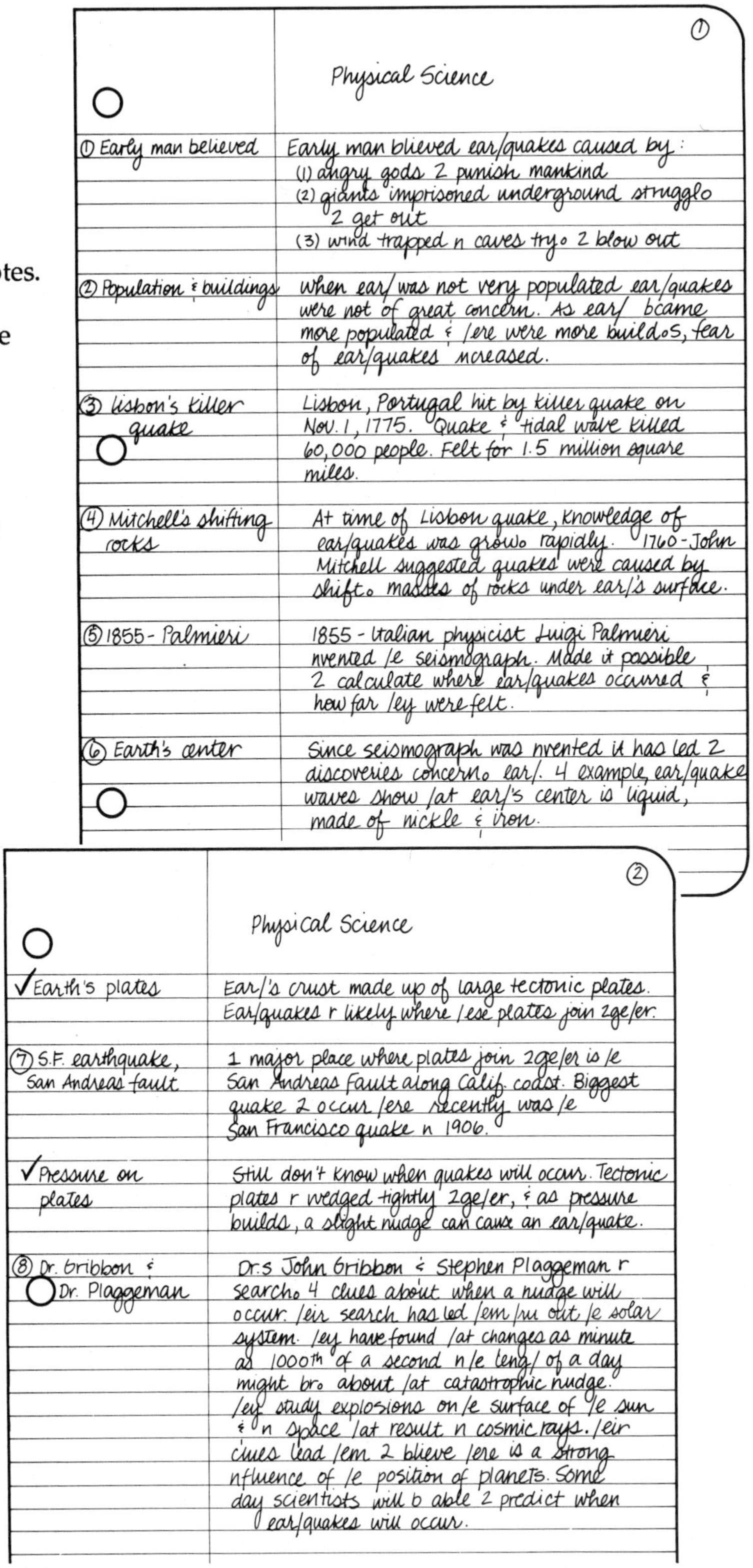

① Physical Science

① Early man believed	Early man blieved ear/quakes caused by: (1) angry gods 2 punish mankind (2) giants imprisoned underground strugglo 2 get out (3) wind trapped n caves tryo 2 blow out
② Population & buildings	When ear/ was not very populated ear/quakes were not of great concern. As ear/ bcame more populated & /ere were more buildos, fear of ear/quakes ncreased.
③ Lisbon's killer quake	Lisbon, Portugal hit by killer quake on Nov. 1, 1775. Quake & tidal wave killed 60,000 people. Felt for 1.5 million square miles.
④ Mitchell's shifting rocks	At time of Lisbon quake, knowledge of ear/quakes was growo rapidly. 1760-John Mitchell suggested quakes were caused by shifto masses of rocks under ear/'s surface.
⑤ 1855-Palmieri	1855 - Italian physicist Luigi Palmieri nvented /e seismograph. Made it possible 2 calculate where ear/quakes occurred & how far /ey were felt.
⑥ Earth's center	Since seismograph was nvented it has led 2 discoveries concerno ear/. 4 example, ear/quake waves show /at ear/'s center is liquid, made of nickle & iron.

② Physical Science

✓Earth's plates	Ear/'s crust made up of large tectonic plates. Ear/quakes r likely where /ese plates join 2ge/er.
⑦ S.F. earthquake, San Andreas fault	1 major place where plates join 2ge/er is /e San Andreas Fault along Calif. coast. Biggest quake 2 occur /ere recently was /e San Francisco quake n 1906.
✓Pressure on plates	Still don't know when quakes will occur. Tectonic plates r wedged tightly 2ge/er, & as pressure builds, a slight nudge can cause an ear/quake.
⑧ Dr. Gribbon & Dr. Plaggeman	Dr.s John Gribbon & Stephen Plaggeman r searcho 4 clues about when a nudge will occur. /eir search has led /em /ru out /e solar system. /ey have found /at changes as minute as 1000th of a second n /e leng/ of a day might bro about /at catastrophic nudge. /ey study explosions on /e surface of /e sun & n space /at result n cosmic rays. /eir clues lead /em 2 blieve /ere is a strong nfluence of /e position of planets. Some day scientists will b able 2 predict when ear/quakes will occur.

Figure 11. Lecture notes used to make Solitaire Lay-Down Cards.

about that same size) for each memory key. In the lecture notes shown in figure 11, there are ten memory keys. However, two memory keys were discarded, so there are eight remaining. Thus you will need eight index cards, one for each memory key.

Write each memory key on a separate card. Copy the memory key onto the card exactly as it is written in the memory key column of your notes. That is, for the first memory key shown in figure 11, you would write on an index card "Early man believed."

Then, in the upper left-hand corner of the index card, write an index number. The index number is made up of the memory key number and the lecture-notes page number. In this example, "Early man believed" is memory key number 1, and it is found on page 1 of the lecture notes. For memory key number 1 on page 1, you would write the index number 1-1 on the index card. Next to the index number you print the letters "LN," meaning "lecture notes." Those letters tell you this is a lecture-note card, not a textbook card.

Finally, you need to add a subject label. This lecture is about earthquakes, so you write the word *earthquakes* next to the index number. Figure 12 shows how your first lecture-note card would look.

Figure 12. A lecture-note card for Solitaire Lay-Down.

This completes all the steps to make one card. If you have your own set of lecture notes for the earthquake lecture, complete with your own personal memory keys, try making a set of cards for those notes to be sure you understand the process. The completed Solitaire Lay-Down Cards from this lecture using the notes shown in figure 11 would look like the examples shown in figure 13. Yours should look similar to this, but with your own memory keys and index numbers.

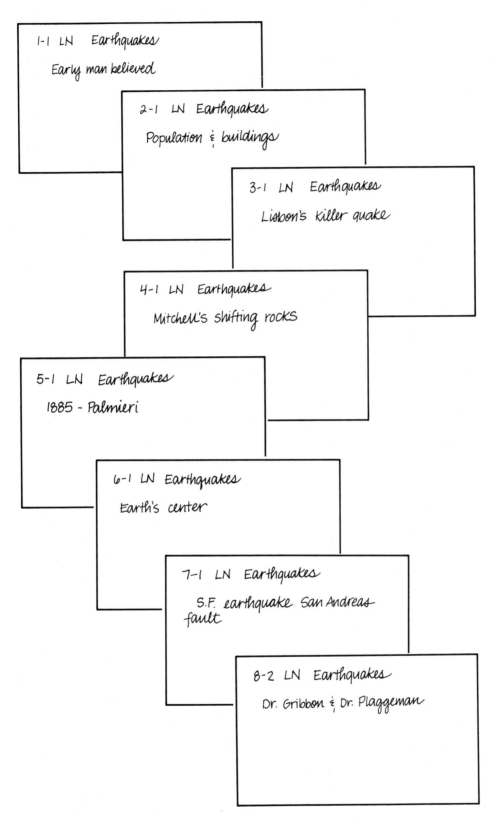

Figure 13. Solitaire Lay-Down Cards for the earthquake lecture.

Step 6.   Use your textbook index cards to complete your deck of Solitaire Lay-Down Cards.

Gather all your textbook index cards from the appropriate section of your textbook. (Of course, you have no textbook notes for the hypothetical situation we have set up, but in a real situation you would.)

Then discard, just as you did with your memory keys. Read each textbook index card very carefully. When you come to a card that covers material you know so well that you are *sure* you don't need to study it further, set the card aside—it is a discard.

Finally, add the remaining textbook index cards to your lecture-note cards. When you combine the cards, you have a full deck of Solitaire Lay-Down Cards.

NOTE: It is very important that you *do not* write answers on the backs of your Solitaire Lay-Down Cards. When you have answers on the backs of your cards, you greatly reduce the effectiveness of this study method. If the answers are too easy for you to refer to, you will read the answers and think you know the material when in fact you do not.

Questions for Discussion

1.   In addition to being an excellent way to study for a test, Solitaire Lay-Down Cards have another advantage. What is that advantage?

2.   What are the six steps in making a deck of Solitaire Lay-Down Cards? Describe what you do for each step.

3.   Why should you never put answers on the backs of your Solitaire Lay-Down Cards?

He that is good for making excuses is good for nothing else.
                              —Benjamin Franklin

Deal Yourself an "A"

Now that you know how to make a complete deck of Solitaire Lay-Down Cards, it's time to learn how to "play" with them. A good player is sure to be a big winner on test day.

Game Rules

1. Shuffle the entire deck of cards. Remember, the full deck includes both your lecture-note cards and your textbook cards. When the deck is shuffled, place it face down in front of you.

2. Begin to play. Turn the top card over. If it's a textbook question, try to answer it based on your knowledge of the textbook. If it's a lecture-note card, try to recall the section of your notes that the memory key refers to.

Whenever you can answer the textbook question, or you get a good readout from the memory key that enables you to recite that section of your lecture notes, then you can turn that card face down in a pile in front of you. If you cannot answer the question or do not get a good readout, lay the card face up in another pile in front of you.

> **NOTE: It is important that you always recite your answers out loud, not silently.** If you recite silently, you may breeze through the deck *thinking* you know the answers when in fact you do not. To be sure you know the material, you must hear yourself say the answers out loud.

3. After you go through the entire deck, you should have two stacks of cards in front of you: A face-down stack of cards with material that you *know*, and a face-up stack of cards with material that you do *not* know.

4. Put face-down cards aside. You already know that material and don't need to study it any more.

5. One by one, review the cards that are face-up. Use the index numbers to refer back to your lecture notes or the textbook to review the material. You need to study this material, but keep in mind that you should not memorize these sections. That may cause a short-circuiting of that wonderful computer-like device called your brain. Just read the material over and be sure you associate the concepts with your memory keys or textbook questions.

6. Reshuffle the cards that stumped you the first time, then begin to play again. Continue to play until you have all the cards face down. At that point, you know the material and are well on your way to an A grade. It's that simple!

Other Ways to Use Solitaire Lay-Down Cards

Although using Solitaire Lay-Down Cards is an excellent way to study for a test alone, it can be equally effective when you study for a test with friends. However, when you study with friends, it is important to remember three guidelines.

1. Limit the study group to a maximum of four students.

2. Make sure each participant in the study group brings his or her own deck of Solitaire Lay-Down Cards to the study session.

3. Make sure each member of the group is dedicated to high-level, intensive study. A study group should not be just an excuse to socialize.

What makes the "group approach" especially effective is that each student brings his or her own special knowledge and understanding of the material to the study session. As a group, you are able to help one another better understand and learn the material.

The following ideas can make the group use of Solitaire Lay-Down Cards both fun and effective.

- Divide the study group into opposing teams. One side uses their combined cards to ask questions that members of the opposing team try to answer.

- Play Elimination. In Elimination, only two members of the group play at one time while the rest of the group watches, listens, and keeps score. Each participant uses his or her own deck of Solitaire Lay-Down Cards to play against the other player. The player with the highest score when all the cards have been played is the winner and takes on the next challenger.

- Play a contest game like Trivial Pursuit or Jeopardy, using the Solitaire Lay-Down Cards to formulate questions.

- Select one member of the group as Study Master. The Study Master uses his or her own deck of Solitaire Lay-Down Cards to quiz other members of the group. The first member of the group who responds correctly to five questions becomes the next Study Master.

Questions for Discussion

1.   Briefly describe the six game rules for playing Solitaire Lay-Down.

2.   Why is it important that you recite the answers out loud when you play Solitaire Lay-Down?

> Life is a series of experiences, each one
> of which makes us bigger, even though
> sometimes it's hard to realize this.
> —Henry Ford

Good Study Methods Prevent the Loser's Limp

You have now learned about a method that can help you prepare for exams. With this method, you will find that the last day or two before an exam are more valuable, perhaps *five times* more valuable, than any other days during a semester. They are more valuable because of the huge amount of high-quality work that you will be doing then—work that can be done only during the last few days before an exam. We're not talking about last-minute cramming; we're talking about the overall review you get through the use of Solitaire Lay-Down Cards.

To do well on a test, you must use the last couple of days prior to the exam to organize and consolidate facts that have been presented. You should not use this time to complete tasks that should have been done previously. When it's time to study for an exam, all your textbook questions and lecture notes should be in perfect order for studying. All your papers should be written and turned in. Your mind should be free to study the material for the exam; you should not be burdened with worry about last-minute details.

"But how do I arrive at this perfect state of readiness?" you might ask. The answer is logical: You do it right the first time.

As the days and weeks pass, you must take notes in every class, using the memory-key method. You must continue to select your memory keys and write them in the memory key

column. Once a week, you should spend five or ten minutes covering up your memory bank and using your memory keys to recall what was said in class. If you do all this, then by test time you will have a notebook full of well-organized, slightly reviewed notes that are ready to be studied in depth.

You must also keep your textbook assignments up-to-date. Your paragraph questions should be written legibly on your index cards, and you should have reviewed them several times. If you have done this, at test time you can review chapters in ten or twenty minutes. If you have *not* done this, you will be forced to go back and reread all the chapters in your textbook.

From the time you take your first notes in class, and from the first paragraph you read in the textbook, you must remember that you are getting ready for an examination. Failure or mediocre performance is inevitable if you fail to do your daily work with an eye toward that ultimate exam.

It is nearly impossible for a student to take a large amount of unorganized, poorly reviewed material and recall enough of it to earn an A or B grade on a test. This is why cramming all night before a test is actually just a terrible punishment for the mind and body. In most cases, the task seems so hopelessly awesome that students give up. Or they may just go through the motions of studying and claim, "I really tried, but I just couldn't learn it all." This excuse is resorting to the loser's limp.

Remember the story about the runner who pulled up with a limp because he needed an excuse for not winning? Well, the limp may have given him an excuse for not winning, but he *still lost.* You too will lose if you resort to excuses rather than preparing ahead of time.

If you have used your time wisely, taken lecture notes in class, selected good memory keys, and read your textbook using the TI-3R method, you will be ready to study for your test. You will be amazed at how easy that task becomes when you use Solitaire Lay-Down Cards. In a study comparing a group of students who used Solitaire Lay-Down Cards with a group who did not, it was determined that, on average, students who used the cards scored 17 points (out of 100) *higher* on tests. As you can see, this could be one of the most useful skills you will ever learn.

Questions for Discussion

1. The day or two before a test is very valuable. What should you be doing during this period?

2. How can you be sure to arrive at a perfect state of readiness to study for a test?

3. Why is failure or mediocre performance inevitable when you do not do your daily work with an eye toward the exam?

4. Why is using Solitaire Lay-Down Cards one of the most useful skills you may ever learn?

Winning is a habit—so is losing.
                                        —Anonymous

Part 6

How to Take Tests

Make no little plans for they have no magic
to stir men's blood. Make big plans. Aim
high in hope and in work.
                                          —Daniel H. Burham

The Splashdown Method for Taking Tests

A typical test is an exercise in which students are required to recall information under pressure. In a survey of 322 junior high and high school tests, it was determined that a student's ability to recall information under pressure was one of the dominant features. Another study revealed that test pressure causes students' pulse rates to increase an average of 30 percent when they are handed a test.

Pressure usually causes tension. Tension can cause you to forget things you once knew. Such memory blocks contribute to low test scores. Therefore, it is very important that you learn how to cope with test pressure.

Test pressure usually begins even before you enter a classroom, as you anticipate the test to come. Then, when you take your seat, the teacher may say something like, "This is the big day. Clear your desks. No more talking." The pressure builds, resulting in increased tension and creating memory blocks.

The teacher hands out the test. If you're a typical student, your pulse rate increases 30 percent. The teacher cautions, "Do not begin until you have read the instructions." More tension, more memory blocks.

You glance through the test. The first thing you see is a question you do not understand. Your palms are sweaty. Your mind frantically attempts to recall important information. The test material that has been so carefully learned becomes jammed. Nothing is coming through. More tension, more memory blocks.

We have all experienced this "logjam" reaction. The turmoil created in a student's mind is much like the jumbled activity that occurs in a logjam on a river. Visualize logs floating peacefully down the river on the way to the sawmill. Suddenly, the river narrows, and the logs must squeeze through a tight channel. There are too many logs trying to rush through at one time. They bump and shove into each other. Some get turned crossways, narrowing the opening still more. More logs pile up until nothing can get through. All the logs are still in the river, but none can get through to the mill.

When you get tense before a test, much the same thing happens in your mind. All the test material you have learned is still in your mind, but it gets jammed up. None of it gets through to where it needs to be: on the test paper.

You must prevent logjamming, a result of tension, from happening. One good way to reduce tension is to keep the information flowing. In order to maintain this flow, you must get the information you have learned onto the test paper as quickly as possible. This is accomplished by using the *Splashdown method*. Splashdown keeps information flowing. It gets information out of your head and onto the paper where you can use it.

Let's take a look at the Splashdown method step by step. We'll start with the moment the teacher hands you a test—that moment when the tension really starts to build.

1. Under no circumstances are you to look at the test paper. Do not even glance at it when the teacher hands it to you. Immediately turn the test face down on your desk.

2. On the back of the test paper, or on a piece of scratch paper if it's permitted, "splash down." Splashing down means simply writing as fast and as furiously as you can all of the terms, phrases, initials, abbreviations, and little memory joggers you can think of. If you are about to take a math test, jot down a few formulas or procedures, or work a quick problem.

This splashdown should take no more than one or two minutes. But when you have completed it, you should have a great deal of information on the back of your test or on scratch paper—information that you can use when it's needed.

3. Turn the test over, read the instructions carefully, then write your name on the paper.

4. Read each question and answer it to the best of your knowledge. Use the splashdown information to help you recall material.

The effectiveness of this method was proven even before it was known as "the Splashdown method." The proving grounds were graduate-level college and university classrooms. Graduate-level students typically are very good at taking tests—they've been doing it for years. In a study, it was noticed that when these students were handed a test, many of them quickly scanned it, then scribbled memory joggers in the margin. After some experimentation, it was discovered that students could improve their test scores if they did not scan the test until *after* they had scribbled their memory joggers. That is to say, when these students were asked to splash down before they looked at the test, their scores improved.

The Splashdown method serves two very useful purposes to you as a test-taker. First, it gives you a ready source of information you can use for reference during a test. Second, the splashdown activity itself—fast and furiously writing your memory joggers—is an excellent way to relieve tension.

Splashdown Examples

To clarify what you do for splashdown, let's look at some simple examples. Consider the following nursery rhyme:

> For want of a nail, the shoe was lost;
> For want of a shoe, the horse was lost;
> For want of a horse, the rider was lost;
> For want of a rider, the battle was lost;
> For want of a battle, the kingdom was lost;
> All for the want of a horseshoe nail.

If you were required to remember the details of this rhyme for a test, your splashdown on the back of the test paper might look like this:

nail-shoe-horse-rider-battle-kingdom

Just these six words could help you recall all the events of the rhyme.

Here's another example. Suppose that for a science test, you need to know the order of the planets in the solar system as well as the following facts:

The asteroid belt divides the solar system into two groups of planets. The inner planets—Mercury, Venus, Earth, and Mars—are thought to have a metal core. The outer planets—Jupiter, Saturn, Uranus, Neptune, and Pluto—are thought to have a rocky core. The inner planets are smaller than the outer planets, except for Pluto, which may be the smallest. Because it doesn't follow the pattern, Pluto is a mystery to scientists. Jupiter is the largest planet with a diameter of 142,800 km—more than 11 times greater than the earth's diameter at 12,756 km. The smallest inner planet is Mercury with a diameter of 4,878 km.

Your splashdown might look like this:

Splashdown Practice Exercises

To become proficient in the use of the Splashdown method, you will need to practice until it becomes almost second nature. When you first begin to use the method, you may feel uncomfortable with it. If that happens, don't be concerned. With continued practice, you will soon feel relaxed and confident for every test. Your improving scores will be welcome evidence that it works.

The following exercises offer some practice in using the Splashdown method. This practice is a little artificial; obviously you aren't usually asked to remember nursery rhymes for a test. To become really proficient at splashdown, you will want to practice on your own, using excerpts from textbooks and other study materials. But try these exercises first to get the general idea.

Exercise 1

Suppose you were expected to remember for a test the beliefs listed in this nursery rhyme. How would you splash down? Jot your ideas on a sheet of paper.

If you sneeze on Monday, you sneeze for danger;
Sneeze on Tuesday, kiss a stranger;
Sneeze on Wednesday, sneeze for a letter;
Sneeze on Thursday, something better;
Sneeze on Friday, sneeze for sorrow;
Sneeze on Saturday, joy tomorrow.

Exercise 2

Suppose you have studied the following facts about Charles Lindbergh and are ready for a test on the information. What memory joggers would you write during splashdown?

On May 20, 1927, a tiny Ryan monoplane took off in the early morning hours from Roosevelt Field, Long Island, New York, carrying a young man whose interest in flying had led him to several years of "barnstorming" throughout the southern and midwestern states. Competing for the prize of $25,000 offered for the first nonstop flight from New York to Paris, Charles Lindbergh had obtained financial backing from a group of St. Louis businessmen. During the next 33 hours and 39 minutes, the lone pilot guided his fragile craft, *The Spirit of St. Louis,* eastward over the ocean. He landed on the evening of May 21 at Le Bourget, Paris, when an anxious world waited to receive the unassuming young man with a tumultuous welcome.

You may wish to compare your splashdown ideas for these exercises with the samples given in the Answer Key on page 145.

Emotional and Physical Preparation for an Exam

There are plenty of myths and conflicting advice about what to do the night before an exam. Some people say you should get up at 3 a.m. the morning of the test to cram. Some think it is better to go to a movie and relax the night before a test. Others say, "Stay up all night and study." There is also differing advice on how to take tests of all kinds—essay tests, standardized tests, and objective tests. Let's consider what happens to you in test situations.

When you use the memory-key method to takes notes in class, use the TI-3R method to read your textbook, and study for the test using your Solitaire Lay-Down Cards, you will know at least 80 to 90 percent of the material that will be on the exam. You will have command of the facts, ideas, and principles you have studied. Even so, you are not guaranteed a good test score unless you are physically and emotionally ready to use your knowledge.

Two vital pieces of equipment must be finely tuned if you expect to do well on an exam. These pieces of equipment are your mind and your body. Lack of sleep and long hours of panicked cramming have a bad effect on these two temperamental tools.

If you don't get enough sleep, chances are you will lack confidence in yourself when you sit down with the test. Fatigue makes cowards of us all, and this can be devastating to your test results. Without rest, you will be unsure about the knowledge you have. This lack of confidence can lower test scores at least 10 percent. In fact, studies have repeatedly shown that a student's confidence can be shaken to the point of failure if he or she is very tired. This failure occurs *even when the student knows the material.*

Witness what happened in an experiment conducted with a class of economics students. In the experiment, students were given a full week of class time to prepare for a rather difficult exam. During the week before the test, students read, reviewed, and were quizzed on the material until they were sure of their ability to pass the test with high scores. One of the stipulations of the experiment was that students had to get at least eight hours of sleep the night before the exam.

On Friday, the students reported that they felt confident as they took the exam. Their confidence was well-founded. The average score on the test was 89.2. Two students scored a perfect 100. No one earned less than a C.

As was planned, after the test the class was invited to a celebration party. The party included refreshments, swimming, volleyball, baseball, badminton, and Ping-Pong. The ground rules for the party required everyone to participate in the enjoyable but exhausting activities until 3:00 a.m. At that hour they went home to sleep until 6:00 a.m. Then they got up and prepared to retake the economics exam at 7:00 a.m. The only difference between the first test and the second test was that the second test was printed on paper of a different color and the questions were in a different sequence. Both tests counted on the students' final grade.

The results of the second test were amazing. The average score on the second test when the students were tired was only 75.4; five people scored low enough to earn a D; and none scored a perfect 100.

Admittedly, this demonstration with a class of 17 students lacked many of the controls of a scientific study, but it demonstrates a valid point: A tired mind and body severely lower your ability to perform well on a test.

Let's analyze why this is true. Picture your body slumped tiredly at your school desk dreading the prospect of taking a test. Your brain is worried because it knows that your body isn't responding well to the directions your brain is sending down. Your body is sluggish, and several malfunctions are becoming increasingly evident.

One malfunction of major concern is the performance of your eyes. They aren't tracking properly because they are sending blurred and faint images to your brain. This is wasting too much valuable time. Your brain is worried that it won't get the information fast enough to finish the test.

Your stomach is also causing concern. It's not a big problem yet, but it could quickly become one. It has a queasy sensation. Your brain has to divide its attention among the stomach discomfort, the problem with your eyes, and concentrating on the test. Your brain's inability to focus attention solely on the test causes your body to fidget and squirm. Frustration becomes overwhelming. Good performance on the test is no longer important. Your consuming desire is to get it over with and go home.

Do you recognize that scenario? Lack of sleep prior to a test is usually the consequence of resolving to accomplish an impossibly large amount of work in a short period of time. As long as you have this self-created mountain of work before you, you will continue to rob yourself of sleep, decent meals, and recreation. The result is that your mind and body end up in poor shape.

The best advice is to get a good night's sleep the night before an exam, even if you haven't prepared well. When you get plenty of sleep, you will at least be able to remember the material you *have* learned.

Some students believe they should set aside studies the night before the exam and attend a relaxing movie. This is poor advice because any activity that comes between the time you learn material and the time you use it will cause you to forget some of what you've learned. Students work too hard and too long to sacrifice some of their learning for a movie. Instead, plan to finish your last study session before the exam with a "grand tour." That is, take all your Solitaire Lay-Down Cards and arrange them by their individual categories and topics to see how each fact fits into the total picture. This final grand tour completes your studying with a panoramic view. After the grand tour, go to bed.

On the morning of the exam, get up early enough so you won't need to rush. A few simple exercises and a shower will freshen you both mentally and physically. Take a last glance at the Solitaire Lay-Down Cards. Eat a satisfying breakfast of good food, not a cup of coffee and a donut. Avoid a breakfast high in sugar content. Studies show that students score significantly lower on tests taken after 10:00 a.m. when they eat a breakfast with high amounts of sugar.

Be aware of your attitude as you go into the test. Attitude is very important. If you take a negative attitude into the classroom with you ("I'm sure I'll flunk," or "I really don't care about this"), your test efforts will be hampered from the start. To do well on an exam you must think positively.

Positive thinking alone will not ensure success, but it really does help. It's called "getting psyched up" for the task at hand. Being mentally psyched up for a mental challenge is just as important as being physically psyched up for a physical challenge.

It's exam time, and you've arrived at the classroom. Make sure you get there early so you can get a good seat—one where the light is good, where the teacher will not disturb you with pacing or rustling papers, and where you can see the chalkboard. In general, sit where there will be a minimum of distractions.

Do not sit near a friend if you can help it. Friends are distractions. Before the exam, any conversation with a friend is likely to break your concentration and disturb the mental attitude you have so painstakingly created. During the exam, both of you are likely to break your concentration if your eyes meet. Toward the end of the exam period, your friend may turn in his or her test paper a bit early. You may feel the temptation to do the same, even if you haven't finished checking over your paper, so that you can follow your friend out of the room and compare notes on the exam.

Once seated in the exam room, you may feel overly tense and anxious. Here are three ways to cope with this exam anxiety:

- Take several slow, deep breaths. As you exhale, let your shoulders drop in a relaxed manner.

- Relax your forehead and jaw muscles, and place your hands loosely on your lap or desk.

- Occupy your mind positively by recalling some of the key questions on your Solitaire Lay-Down Cards. Say to yourself, "The knowledge is all stored in my mind, and I am prepared and capable of doing well on this test."

Questions for Discussion

1. How can you be sure you will know at least 80 to 90 percent of the material that will be on an exam?

2. What two pieces of equipment must be finely tuned if you intend to do well on an exam?

3. What did the experiment with a class of economics students reveal?

4. What usually causes students to miss sleep the night before an exam?

5. What should you do the night before an exam to help you complete your studying?

6. What should you do the morning of the exam?

7. What can you do when you arrive in the classroom to improve your chances of earning a good grade?

8. What can you do to cope with exam anxiety?

> **It doesn't necessarily take great minds to do great things—dedication works just about as well.**
> **—Anonymous**

Improving Concentration During a Test

William James, a philosopher and psychologist, said, "Some new thought or idea tries to gain our attention every two or three seconds. These thoughts and ideas are constantly knocking on the door of our mind, trying to get attention." If a new thought or idea comes to mind every two or three seconds, it's easy to understand why you may experience difficulty trying to remember everything there is to remember during an exam.

Most students would agree that improved concentration would be beneficial during a test. Unfortunately, it is ridiculously easy to lose concentration. For example, suppose you are in the middle of a test, thinking hard about the answer to a question. Suddenly you realize how deeply you're concentrating. At that moment, you have broken your concentration.

William James said, "Trying to seize concentration is like trying to turn on the light quickly enough to see the darkness, or trying to grab a spinning top to look at its motion." We all know that neither of these things is possible. It is the same with concentration. Concentration only occurs when you don't think about it.

Even though concentration is very elusive, anything you can do to maximize it will improve your test scores. By focusing your total attention on the exam and turning interruptions into occasions that will inspire you to greater effort, you will have a much better chance of earning a high test score.

What is the single most distracting thing that can happen during an exam to destroy your concentration? What most often causes discouragement? The answer to both of these questions is *worry*.

Let's analyze what happens when you worry. When you are worried, you form a disturbing mental picture of what will happen if you should fail. Worrying causes deep, troubling feelings. Those feelings nag at you—they won't leave you alone. The thought of failure becomes so strong in your mind that you begin to believe it's inevitable. You live the failure before it happens. With such troubling mental images distracting you, it's no wonder you have difficulty concentrating on an exam. The negative thoughts are so strong that they block out the facts you learned while studying for the test.

How can you erase the negative feelings caused by worry? You must completely reverse the thought process and picture yourself successfully passing the test. You must force yourself to anticipate the best possible outcome and arouse in yourself a deep desire to earn a good grade. Be inspired by what will happen once you successfully pass the test. Keep going over it in your mind. Remember, your negative beliefs about failure were formed by thoughts and vivid mental pictures of failure. You must fill your mind with new positive thoughts about what it will be like to earn a high score; that way positive mental pictures will erase old negative thoughts. You must inflate your confidence and let it soar until you want to succeed more than anything else.

Positive thoughts alone will not guarantee success. However, a positive mental picture will encourage you to put out the extra effort that's needed if you are to earn a high test score.

The methods just described will not eliminate the new thoughts that try to get your attention every two or three seconds. However, the thoughts that do enter your mind will be positive and encouraging ones. These thoughts will help spur you on to better performance instead of discouraging and distracting you.

Questions for Discussion

1. What did William James say about new thoughts? How can these thoughts break your concentration?

2. Explain this statement: "Concentration only occurs when you do not think about it."

3. Why does worrying make it difficult to concentrate on an exam?

4. How can a positive attitude help you do well on a test?

5. If the methods described in this section will not totally prevent new thoughts and ideas from trying to get your attention, how will they help you score higher on a test?

Every person has an equal chance to become better than they are.
                                                    —Anonymous

Objective Tests: Plan Your Strategy

Teachers give different kinds of tests, and you need to approach them in different ways. One kind is called an *objective test*. An objective test might include true-false questions, multiple-choice questions, and short-answer questions. Objective tests may be either teacher-constructed or standardized. A teacher-constructed test is made up by your teacher or by a group of teachers at your school. Standardized tests, on the other hand, come from major textbook publishers or special testing companies.

The following suggestions for taking objective tests are applicable to both teacher-constructed and standardized tests. However, standardized tests often have separate answer sheets that are machine-scored. When this is the case, you must follow the test directions very carefully, especially if they tell you to use a certain type of pencil or if they specify a particular method for marking your answers.

The first thing you do when the teacher hands you an objective test, as with any other type of test, is splash down. The next step, a very important one, is *read the directions carefully.* You might know the subject material perfectly, but if you are careless about following directions, you could still fail the test. Yes, REALLY. Before you start to do the test, ask yourself questions like these: "Can I answer with sentence fragments, or must the answers be expressed in complete sentences? If there is a list of terms to choose from, can I use any term more than once?" The test directions will give you the answers to such questions. Paying attention to these directions is vital to getting a good score.

An objective test is usually constructed in such a way that you will need the entire class period to complete it. In fact, you may need to work quickly in order to finish. Since time is critical, you should plunge ahead as soon as you have the test in hand, but do so intelligently. Follow this sequence and you'll stay out of trouble:

1. **Splash down.**

2. **Read the directions** carefully.

3. **Skim the exam** to become familiar with the types of questions asked.

4. **Notice the weights assigned to specific questions.** That is, are some questions worth 2 points each, others worth 5 or 10 points each? If you think you might be short of time, be sure to spend the most time on the questions that will give you the most points.

5. **Establish a time plan for successful completion of the test.** To help you stick to the plan, make time notations in the margin of the test paper. For example, if the exam begins at 10:00, and you think you need to complete question 12 by 10:15, write 10:15 next to question 12. Next to each segment of the test, write the time that coincides with your time plan. When you establish your time plan, be sure to allow enough time to review your answers and reconsider any questionable answers.

Don't let yourself get stuck. If a question slows you down, mark it and go on to the next question. Come back to difficult questions later. You will pick up more points by sticking to your time plan than by wasting time puzzling over a difficult question.

If you think a particular question has two possible answers, place a mark in the margin indicating that you should come back to it later. Before you go on, place a faint mark next to the answer you think is most likely the correct one. You will then avoid having to go through the original reasoning process again when you return to think about the question more carefully.

When you go back through the test, don't be afraid to change an answer if you have given your change careful consideration. Studies indicate that students who change their original answers after careful consideration *do* increase their scores.

You must assume that the teacher will not give you trick questions unless past experience has proven otherwise. If you adopt a skeptical attitude, you will tend to read too much into each question and waste needless time looking for the trick. Of course, some true-false or multiple-choice questions, hinging on the accuracy of a single detail, may seem like tricks to the unprepared student. But if you are well prepared, you should be able to see what the question is getting at. As a general rule, read each question carefully, then concentrate on the main point of the question without getting sidetracked by unimportant details.

Questions for Discussion

1. What is the best sequence to follow when you begin to take an objective test?

2. How can you help yourself stick to your time plan?

3. What should you do if you get stuck on a question?

4. What should you do if you think a question has two possible answers?

5. What do studies indicate about students who change original answers?

> I never did anything worth doing by accident; nor did any of my inventions come by accident; they came by work.
> —Thomas A. Edison

Essay Tests: Students Have the Advantage

In general, as you advance through school, you will find teachers at the higher levels giving fewer objective tests and more essay tests. An essay test is a special challenge. It asks you to pull ideas and facts out of your head without the aid that a true-false or multiple-choice question can give you. Many students are intimidated by essay tests, but think about it for a moment. You are actually more in control with essay questions.

How are you in control? Let's take a minute to think about objective tests. When teachers make up such tests, they formulate the questions based on their knowledge of the subject. They write each question with a specific answer in mind, and they will be looking for exactly that answer from you. You probably don't have exactly the same perspective on the subject that your teacher does. When you read the question, it may trigger a response in your mind that's different from the one the teacher is looking for. Maybe your answer is not technically wrong, but chances are it will be marked wrong if it doesn't exactly match the answer the teacher wants.

An essay question eliminates this problem. The teacher may still be looking for a particular response to the question, but even if your response is slightly different, you have the chance to get your point across and earn at least partial credit. Do not fear the essay test! See it as an opportunity to pick up some extra points—points that you might have lost on an objective test, where each question has only one possible answer and you have no chance to explain your views.

Effective essay answers contain specific facts and ideas, but they also are written in organized, thoughtful, and forceful sentences and paragraphs. Sometimes in your effort to write good, forceful sentences, you may lose some of the facts and ideas. This is an excellent reason to use the Splashdown method for essay tests. Always use the back of the exam sheet, as soon as it's handed to you, to quickly splash down facts, ideas, and details that you think you might forget—summarizing the material you studied before you even read the exam questions. Splashdown is a positive action that involves you in the exam immediately; it gets you started. Think of your splashdown information as a reference library; you might even think of it as "honest cheat notes." Just be careful not to take too long to splash down, never more than one or two minutes.

After you splash down, it's always important to read the directions carefully and be sure you understand them. Too many students have done poorly on an exam because they attempted to answer all six essay questions listed when the instructions clearly stated, "Choose **three** of the six questions."

After you read the directions carefully, read all the essay questions before you attempt to answer any of them. By reading all the questions, you won't make the mistake of overwriting; that is, you won't answer one question with information that could be better used in your response to another question.

While you are reading the questions, quickly jot down in the margin next to each question a few words, ideas, and phrases that come to mind. With these ideas and your splashdown on the back, you should feel confident about having something to say on each question.

Time, an important factor in any exam, is particularly crucial in an essay exam. Be sure to establish a realistic time plan so that you don't spend 40 minutes on one question and 5 minutes each on two others. Of course, if one question is worth more points than the others, it will probably pay to allot more time to that answer. If you do run out of time in spite of careful planning, don't panic. Quickly jot down an outline of your remaining ideas to show the teacher that you do, in fact, know the answer. Doing this will often gain you points, even though your ideas are not carefully written out.

After you have read all the questions and established a time plan, begin to write your answers. Always start with the easiest questions. This will get you off and running, and nothing gives you confidence faster than a good running start. As you complete your essay for each question, be sure to leave some space on your paper; this will give you a place to write any additional ideas that may occur to you later on. The content of your essay answer should demonstrate two things: first, that you understand the question, and second, that you know the material well enough to answer the question. You can best demonstrate these two things if you have a well-organized answer filled with concrete facts and ideas.

A well-organized answer always begins by getting right to the point. Do not start an essay answer with a glorious, wordy introduction or with space-filling sentences such as, "I think this is an excellent question, and the answer deserves a lot of deep thought and consideration. Therefore, I would like to state . . ."

Beginning your response with such empty statements just wastes precious time. You may glance back over such an answer and think, "Gee, I really wrote a lot on that question," but the only person you impress is yourself. Teachers are not interested in what you think about the quality of the question. They are interested in whether or not you understand and can answer it.

The direct approach is always the best way to answer an essay question. The key to giving a direct answer is to partially repeat the question and make it the beginning of your answer. You then develop the essay from this statement. For example, suppose the question is, "What were the three most important economic factors of the 1920s?" You might begin your answer with, "The three most important economic factors of the 1920s were . . ." This approach leads you directly to the point and clearly demonstrates that you know the answer. You save time and effort because you are forced to organize your answer into a direct, concise response.

Questions for Discussion

1.   Why are students actually in more control with essay tests than with objective tests?

2.   Why is splashdown important for an essay test?

3.   Why should you read all the questions before answering any of them?

4.   Why is it best to start an essay exam with the easiest question?

5.   What is the direct approach to answering an essay question?

6.   What can you do on an essay test if you run out of time before you have finished writing your answers? How can you help avoid running out of time?

Don't get angry at someone who knows more than you do; it's not his fault.
—Anonymous

Your Corrected Test Is Valuable

Regardless of the type of test, be it multiple-choice, short-answer, or essay, your corrected paper can be a valuable guide for learning after it is returned to you. Don't throw it away; it holds clues that will help you do better on the next exam. You may feel tempted to never look at it again, especially if you got a low grade. But take a few minutes to analyze your strengths and weaknesses. Look for ways you can improve your performance on future tests. This analysis, done under "non-crisis" conditions, can also be a good way to etch the material still more deeply into your long-term memory.

If your score is not as high as you would have liked, don't spend a lot of time being depressed. Recognize your errors, analyze them, and learn how to correct them. Above all, study any comments made by the teacher. If you have questions about the test, by all means ask for clarification. Don't be embarrassed. You may find that your problem is not knowing *how* to take a particular teacher's examinations rather than not knowing the test material.

The most impressive thing you can do in any course is to show steady progress. Few teachers give a final grade based on a cumulative average. The last examination in a course is usually far more important than the first. For example, if you were a teacher, to which of the following students would you give the higher final grade? Judy starts with an 85 percent, dips to 75 percent, rises slightly to 80 percent, and in her final exam staggers through with 67 percent. Gary fails his first test with 40 percent, pulls up to 75 percent on the next test, then to 80 percent, and is a class leader with a 92 percent on his final. Strictly speaking, Judy has the higher average (Judy, 76.75; Gary, 71.75), but you can bet most teachers would give Gary the higher grade. Steady progress reflects credit on both the student and the teacher.

Questions for Discussion

1.   How can your corrected test be a valuable guide for learning?

2.   What should you do if your score is not as high as you would have liked?

> **Courage is not something you lose.**
> **Courage is always an option.**
> —R. H. Schuller

The Beginning

You probably think it's strange to end a book with "the beginning," but after all, this is a book that started with "the end." Besides, your completion of *How to Study* is indeed a beginning—the beginning of a brighter academic career.

In reading this book you have learned about five valuable study skills:

1.   **How to manage your time.**   You now know how to prepare a daily, prioritized schedule, allowing yourself goof-off time as well as the study time you need. You also know to break long tasks into smaller, more manageable chunks.

2. How to listen and take notes in class. You know how to use common-sense speed writing as you jot down class notes. You also know about the memory-key method, in which you take notes on paper divided into two columns and later add memory keys in the recall column to help you study and learn the material presented in class.

3. How to study a textbook. The main tool you have learned here is the TI-3R method: Think, Index, Read, Record, Recite. If you follow this approach, you end up with a valuable collection of note cards to help you study and learn the material presented in the book.

4. How to study for tests. You know how to make a Solitaire Lay-Down deck, using your textbook note cards and making additional cards based on your class notes. Then you know how to play Solitaire Lay-Down until you feel confident that you know the material.

5. How to take a test. You've learned that it's important to be emotionally prepared and to go into the test with a positive attitude. You also know how to use the Splashdown method to prevent tension and mental blocks, and you have learned how to avoid some common pitfalls on both objective tests and essay tests.

These skills are tools, and like other tools, they are meant to be used. Just as a lawn mower will not benefit anyone's lawn if the tool sits idle in the garage, neither will your study skills benefit your grades if you leave everything you've learned within the pages of this book. Use these tools, and you will realize amazing results.

> **You must never, never, never, quit.**
> **—Winston Churchill**

Answer Key

Part 3   How to Take Notes in Class

Page 42, Exercise 1

1. be	7. you	13. any
2. for	8. are	14. happy
3. before	9. you are	15. sad
4. in	10. inform	16. are you in?
5. to	11. forward	17. Indian
6. into	12. see	18. easy

19. I c u b4 u c me.

Page 42, Exercise 2

1. /ey	7. /ere4	13. bro/er
2. /at	8. wi/	14. mo/er
3. /en	9. bo/	15. ra/er
4. /is	10. 2/	16. 2ge/er
5. /ose	11. fa/er	17. ano/er
6. /e	12. o/er	18. bo/er

Page 43, Exercise 3

1. /o	4. no/o
2. some/o	5. /oS
3. every/o	6. ne/o

Page 43, Exercise 4

1. go₀
2. do₀
3. want₀
4. open₀
5. runn₀
6. walk₀

7. learn₀
8. talk₀
9. jump₀
10. eat₀
11. /ink₀
12. no/₀

13. /₀
14. some/₀
15. n4m₀
16. c₀
17. b₀
18. r u n

Page 44, Exercise 5

1. b
2. bcame
3. 4
4. b4
5. 2
6. 2ge/er

7. n
8. nvented
9. ncrease
10. /an
11. /ere
12. blieve

13. ne
14. wi/
15. ear/
16. ez
17. bcause
18. /ey r n

Page 44, Exercise 6

1. they
2. that
3. them
4. this
5. those
6. the
7. with

8. both
9. father
10. other
11. brother
12. mother
13. rather
14. together

15. another
16. tooth
17. something
18. everything
19. nothing
20. things
21. anything

22. informing
23. seeing
24. being
25. walking
26. eating
27. wanting
28. thinking

Pages 58-60, Lectures 1 through 4

Answers will vary somewhat but should be similar to the samples shown.

Lecture 1.

Memory Keys	Facts About the Moon
	Notes
Closer but smaller	Moon appears larger /an sun & stars only bcause it's closer 2 ear/
200,000 miles - 64 hrs.	Moon - 200,000 miles from ear/. Takes spaceships about 64 hrs 2 get 2 moon.
Long days - no pets	Days & nights on moon r 2 weeks long. Days r very hot - nights cold bcause no air on moon. No plants or animals.
No need for diets	Gravity 1/6 of ear/s. 120 lb. person would weigh only 20 lbs.

Lecture 2.

memory Keys	Christopher Columbus
	Notes
Little round world 500 years ago	Columbus born about 500 years ago n Genoa Italy. He blieved world was round & much smaller /an it is.
England, Portugal no, Spain sí	Wanted 2 sail 2 India by sailo west. Kings of Portugal and England refused help. After 7 yrs. of asko Isabella and Ferdinand of Spain gave him ships & men.
1492	Never reached India but found America n 1492.

Lecture 3.

memory Keys	the Dragonfly Notes
Dragonfly described	Dragonfly has 4 wings, long slender body, many eyes, can c all directions at once.
Swamps & insects	Lives n swamps & still water. Eats insects - mostly mosquitoes
Eggs - babies - adults	Female Dflies lay eggs on water & on water plants. Hatch n 2 weeks. Babies live n water 1-5 yrs. Skin changes many times until /ey become adults & leave water.

Lecture 4.

Memory Keys	Listening and hearing
	Notes
E = hearing	Hearo not same as listeno. — we hear w/
E+M+F = listening	our ears, but must use our ears, mind
	& feelo5 2 listen.
Listening requires	Listeno involves 4 /os : 1) attention,
A + H + U & R	2) hearo, 3) understando, 4) remembero
Stone wall	If we only hear & don't listen we're like
	stone wall. (what goes n 1 ear comes out
	/e o/er - might as well b talko 2 a
	stone wall)

Part 6   How to Take Tests

Page 121, Exercise 1

Answers will vary but might be similar to this:

Mon. - danger
Tues. - stranger
Wed. - letter
Thurs. - better
Fri. - sorrow
Sat. - joy

Page 121, Exercise 2

Answers will vary but might be similar to this:

5/20/27 left Roos. Field N.Y.
$ 25,000
N.Y. to Paris 33 hrs. 39 min.
Le Bourget Field 5/21/27